WEST OVER THE WAVES

The Final Flight of Elsie Mackay

JAYNE BALDWIN

2QT Limited (Publishing)

Revised 3rd edition 2017

2QT Limited (Publishing)
Settle
North Yorkshire
BD24 9RH
United Kingdom

Photographs supplied by Jayne Baldwin
Front Cover Image: Elsie Mackay in a Sidcot flying suit

Printed in Great Britain by Lightning Source UK

Previous edition ISBN 978-1872350240 published by GC Book
Publishers Ltd

A CIP catalogue record for this book is available
from the British Library
ISBN 978-1-912014-69-9

For my father Jack Baldwin DFC

Contents

Introduction

Just before dawn on March 13th 1928 a beautiful young earl's daughter looked out into the darkness from her hotel room. She had barely slept after spending a restless night wrestling with her conscience. News had leaked out of her association with the famous one-eyed pilot Captain W. G. R. Hinchliffe and there were rumours about the real destination of their small plane, in which they had been carrying out long test flights above the Lincolnshire countryside. National newspapers had been filled with frenzied speculation about the captain's preparations, reporters asking questions such as who was going to fly? Were they planning an overland flight to India, or were the stories true that they were instead attempting the treacherous east–west crossing of the Atlantic, something that had never been achieved before?

The headlines had been full of triumphs and tragedies for months; it was as if the world had aviation fever. So many experienced flyers had been lost, including two women who had disappeared without trace. The Honourable Elsie Mackay claimed her only interest in the venture was as a financial backer but it was feared that she held a burning ambition to be the first woman to fly the Atlantic.

Leaving the hotel wrapped in a scarf and furs in an attempt to disguise her flying clothes, Elsie slid into the back seat of her silver Rolls Royce and asked her driver to take her to the church, where she took communion and knelt quietly in prayer. The priest saw tears in her eyes and tried to counsel her but, with a wave of her hand, she left to travel the few short miles to the RAF airfield where the small monoplane the *Endeavour* waited.

Snow still covered the runway; wintry storms had held up their plans to take off for more than a week and permission to use the aerodrome had run out – the plane had to be moved. Only a handful of people saw Elsie and Captain Hinchliffe climb into the cockpit and fewer still knew about the months of extensive planning carried out in the utmost secrecy. Filled with fuel for a long-distance flight, the plane rumbled heavily along the runway before finally lifting into the air to disappear forever into the clouds.

Elsie Mackay - her pilot's license photograph.
(image courtesy of the Royal Aero Club Trust, UK)

CHAPTER ONE

Not for Fame or Fortune

For a few fleeting hours in March 1928 it seemed as if everybody in the British Isles and along the eastern seaboard of North America held their breath, faces upturned, eyes searching the skies, each person willing the small Stinson Detroiter plane and its two brave flyers safely across the waves. Most of the world appeared to be in the grip of Atlantic Fever – an obsession with the new and exciting science of flight and, in particular, the challenge of flying the ocean between Europe and the Americas.

From a tiny village on the south-west coast of Scotland to a Mayfair townhouse in London, from a Lincolnshire airfield to the fishing ports of Newfoundland and an aerodrome in Philadelphia, people were waiting for news of the *Endeavour*. Would this flight succeed where so many others had failed? The whole venture had, unusually, been shrouded in mystery; at first no one was sure who was on board the plane or where they were heading. Rumours and counter-rumours raged across newspaper headlines until it was finally confirmed that the dashing one-eyed pilot Captain W. G. R. Hinchliffe had been joined in the cockpit by the glamorous heiress Elsie Mackay, the wayward daughter of shipping tycoon Lord Inchcape. They were attempting to enter the history books as the first to fly the Atlantic from east to west; this would also be a first flight in either direction for a woman.

By the time the news reporters had ascertained who exactly was on board the Stinson Detroiter and where it was heading, it was also becoming far too clear that the flight was overdue. The story of the Atlantic attempt by Captain W. G. R. Hinchliffe and the Honourable Elsie Mackay ended in the same way that it had started – shrouded in mystery. To this day no one knows exactly what happened to the two intrepid aviators; only that their flight was, in time, added to the annals of aviation history under the chapter heading 'Flights to Nowhere'.

A month later a German-Irish attempt on the same treacherous route would prove to be successful and only a few months passed before the American aviator Amelia Earhart claimed the title of the first woman to cross the Atlantic. This initial success, sitting in the back of the Fokker trimotor called *The Friendship*, established Miss Earhart's aviation career but the women who shared her dream of claiming the Atlantic crown have largely been forgotten. Amongst them was the extraordinary Elsie Mackay.

The American's success, so closely on the heels of Miss Mackay's failure, combined with a strange tale of the supernatural that followed the name of Captain Hinchliffe, helped to overshadow Elsie's courage, determination and skill as a pilot. Her story, though, is a fascinating one and deserves more attention than simply being a footnote to Captain Hinchliffe's adventures before and after death. Certainly in 1928 the mention of Elsie's name had people enthralled on both sides of the Atlantic. Revelatory headlines concerning the flight were all the more shocking because of the secrecy and mystery surrounding the preparations. This led many critics to claim that Hinchliffe and Mackay were ill-prepared for such a dangerous undertaking and that the whole thing had been nothing but a rich woman's whimsy. Yet in 1936 an article in the *Sunday Graphic and Sunday News* stated that: 'At the time it was made there were many who said that the Honourable Elsie Mackay's attempt was foolhardy and embarked upon without adequate preparation. This is entirely contrary to the facts.'

In those early days of aviation pioneering, pilots were big news. This was the cutting edge of technology, surrounded by the same kind of glamour and excitement that would be a feature of the first missions to reach the moon decades later. The adventures of these early aviators were followed by the public with great interest; not only were these intrepid men and women in their flying machines pushing forward the boundaries of science but they made great copy for newspaper reporters. Big money prizes, tragedy, rivalries and the many thrills and spills meant that articles about aviators and their escapades were never far from the front page. Record attempts ended in failure and crossing the Atlantic proved to be a particularly fatal attraction for many experienced flyers who wanted to be the first.

In 1913, only ten years after the Wright brothers made history by flying 120 feet in a powered heavier-than-air craft, the race to fly across the Atlantic was fuelled by the announcement from the Northcliffe-owned newspaper, *The Daily Mail* that a prize of £10,000 would be paid 'to the first person who crosses the Atlantic from any point in the United States, Canada, or Newfoundland to any point in Great Britain or Ireland in 72 continuous hours'. The remarkable achievement by Alcock and Brown in 1919 did nothing to stem the flood of would-be flyers intent on conquering the thousands of miles of unforgiving waves. The promise of further prizes meant that there was always someone new ready to take on the challenge, despite a rising death toll.

The Honourable Elsie Mackay was not attracted to this dangerous adventure by the promise of the kind of fame and fortune that later greeted Amelia Earhart for she already had both. It was her glamorous reputation, her brief career as a cinema actress, her pioneering position as a designer of ship interiors and her place in British high society that led to an even greater interest in her flying ambitions than would otherwise have been the case. But, unlike every other aviator at the time, Elsie was not seeking publicity; in fact, she desperately wanted to keep her dream of flying the Atlantic a secret. She knew that her father, the shipping magnate Lord Inchcape, would do everything in his power to thwart her ambition – and he had the power and influence to stop her.

Elsie Mackay was born into a life of wealth and privilege thanks to the extraordinary drive and character of her father, who, by the time Elsie started taking flying lessons in the early 1920s, was one of the most influential businessmen in the British Empire. Shortly after her Atlantic attempt he was created the First Earl of Inchcape, though he began life as plain James Lyle Mackay.

His life began in Arbroath in 1852, the third of five children born to James

Mackay and Deborah Lyle. His father was a master mariner, the owner and captain of a number of barques including the *Seafield*, *Eliot* and *Witch of the Waves* – ships that brought cargos of flax from the Russian port of Archangel bound for the rope and canvas works in Arbroath, carried corn from New Orleans to Galway during the potato famine and took Irish emigrants across the Atlantic to Halifax, Nova Scotia. It was in this Canadian port that James Mackay senior had met his future wife, Deborah.

To mark his eighth birthday, James Lyle Mackay was allowed to accompany his father on a voyage to Archangel for the first time – but it was a journey that almost proved to be his last. The small boy had to be saved twice from drowning after falling overboard from the three-hundred-ton barque, the *Asia*, the first time by a young Russian sailor and the second by the ship's cook. Despite this hair-raising introduction to life aboard ship, a love of seafaring and yachting stayed with Lord Inchcape for the rest of his life.

Only two years later James Mackay senior was drowned at the age of forty after being thrown into the sea on a voyage across the Atlantic in the ship *Seafield*, a terrible fate that echoed through the family. Lord Inchcape would be haunted by the loss not only of his father but of two uncles who also succumbed to the same watery grave; of course, his favourite daughter would also lose her life trying to cross this unforgiving expanse of ocean and, in all likelihood, met the same fate.

James was just ten years old when his father drowned. When his mother died later the same year, he was sent away to school, his elder brother having already started his own career at sea. The boy who was to achieve such greatness in later years and who was to be rewarded with accolades, title and status for his business acumen and public service made a very poor start in his school life. He attended Arbroath Academy and the prestigious Elgin Academy, though his education was scanty and he would later admit that he had not been an ideal pupil. James was described as a 'wild truant' who was happier hanging around the harbour or poaching salmon. He would later describe himself as 'fonder of boats than books, I was a forward sort of boy ... extremely naughty ... who would never come to any good. Eventually I was brought to heel by four years of the strict discipline of an office.'

Despite being 'idle and lazy' by his own admission, his saving grace was his handwriting and it was this skill that led to his being given a job as a scrivener in a solicitors' office in Arbroath after leaving school at the age of fourteen. Within a year he left to join an Arbroath rope and canvas manufacturer – a job that took him closer to the sea. He earned five pounds in his first year of office life, regularly working each day from nine in the morning to eight o'clock at night, though it was frequently as late as ten or eleven o'clock before he left. This energy and ability to work long hours would later be seen in the brief career of his daughter Elsie.

Setting his sights further than the harbour walls of Arbroath, at the age of twenty-two James joined the customs department of Gellatly, Hankey and Sewell in London, before going into the service of the trading company

James Mackay, the first Earl of Inchcape.
(photograph courtesy of William Barraclough)

Mackinnon, Mackenzie and Co, the agents of the British India Steamship Navigation Company. He travelled to India to represent the firm there and made his mark as an assistant in the Bombay office. On a critical occasion when the local manager was absent, a crisis occurred; 'acting with ruthless brilliance', the young Mackay saved the day, upholding the reputation of the company and preventing serious loss. After this, the man who later described himself as a 'humble box-wallah' rose rapidly in the company; it wasn't long before he was taken into partnership and became the Calcutta manager of the British India Steam Navigation Company.

Throughout his life Lord Inchcape was blessed with robust health and an endless store of energy but, after seven years in India, a bout of typhoid fever took him back to Scotland to recuperate. It was during this return home to Arbroath that he met his future wife, Jane Paterson Shanks.

According to *The Times's* obituary written on the death of Lord Inchcape, 'the escapades of his boyhood included some unauthorised visits in small craft to the Inchcape rock with his friend and companion Jane Paterson Shanks whom he married in 1883 and who exercised a wise and gracious influence over his career. When he was raised to the peerage in 1911 as Lord Inchcape of Strathnaver she heartily approved of his choice of the title Inchcape and so did the Commissioners of the Northern Lights.'

Jane returned with him to India and the four eldest children, including Elsie, were born there. She was still an infant when the family returned to Britain in 1893 and her sister Effie was born in London the following year.

James Lyle Mackay had made such an impression whilst in India that, when he left, the newspaper *The Englishman* featured a lengthy article about his achievements. In conclusion it stated that: 'Mr Mackay leaves India as a merchant called to take his place in the home office of his firm, and yet he also leaves it as a leader of the general community whose guidance is acknowledged on all sides, and who, not being a paid servant of the state has yet come to be regarded as one of the foremost public servants of India.' But this was only the beginning.

Branching out into shipping in the Far East, James Mackay became an authority on oriental trade. In 1902 he was appointed by the British government to be the King's Special Commissioner and Plenipotentiary in order to negotiate a vital commercial agreement with China, an agreement that became known as the Mackay Treaty. He went on to be appointed chairman of the British India Steam Navigation Company, by then the biggest British-owned shipping company in the world, which merged in 1911 with the Peninsular and Orient Company, more familiar as P&O. Within weeks of this appointment as the managing director of the new organisation, James Mackay oversaw the sailing of twenty-four of his ships from India to France; a transportation of thirty thousand officers and men that was the largest troop movement ever carried out in one convoy.

The many and varied achievements of this great life are too considerable to be listed here but they were told in the biography of Lord Inchcape written by Hector Bolitho in 1936, authorised by Inchcape's widow, Jane. After his death in 1932, *The Manchester Guardian* obituary writer said: 'Few of the British Empire's prominent businessmen ever controlled so many varied commercial interests as the Earl of Inchcape did during his long life, and fewer still, perhaps, gave so generously of their time and labour to the service of the community. In shipping, commerce and finance he was pre-eminent and the soundness and efficiency of the undertakings with which he was connected testify today to his exceptional administrative skill, native shrewdness, courage and wide and deep knowledge of men and affairs.'

In the months following his daughter's disappearance, Lord Inchcape was frequently described by the press as severe; he could, on occasion, be very stern. According to *The Guardian*: 'when he made up his mind there was very little more to be said. But the sternness of the administrator really concealed a rather kindly human being with a keen sense of humour.' *The Times* echoed these sentiments, saying: 'his ambition was controlled by Scottish caution and tempered by a keen sense of humour and a warm heart and a zest for play as well as for work. In his speeches he was renowned for saying exactly what he thought and meaning exactly what he said. As head of P&O and British India companies Lord Inchcape's work began when many ordinarily active men were still sleeping; but if he worked hard, his zest for sport and social intercourse was no less intense. He was a good yachtsman and fisherman and a good shot. He had an unfailing sense of humour and a disarming smile and his range of friendships included a vast number of people of all conditions in life from the King and Queen to his humblest members of staff.'

One of his Indian clerks, Shivram Ramchandra, told biographer Hector Bolitho that Lord Inchcape had a 'nobleness of heart which won for him the loyalty of the Indian employees whom he had the goodness to look upon as friends more than employees'. Whilst being very shrewd, tough and determined, he was also a kind and generous person who was ever reluctant to show this side of his character to the outside world – it would not have been good for business. One particular story that was repeated through the generations of the Mackay family is that when he was chairman of P&O, he encouraged fellow directors to attend meetings by leaving a small bag of gold sovereigns at each place. Absentees forfeited the gold, which was then shared out amongst those at the table.

As Lord Inchcape and his siblings had lost their parents at a young age, it appears that he took on the role of watchful, protective old brother, particularly towards his youngest sister Annie Mackay. She was in Calcutta staying with her brother when she met the city's harbour master, Henry Brereton Hooper, a former India Marine captain. A relationship soon developed but Anna's brother disapproved of the young Hooper and, initially, did not feel he was suitable to marry his sister; a similar situation would arise in Elsie's life when she fell in love. In Anna's case, the gallant captain must have eventually made a good impression because the couple married and Hooper was rewarded with the positions of managing director and vice-chairman of the General Steam Navigation Company, part of the Inchcape shipping empire. Their daughter Maude Lyle Hooper, known to the family as Bluebell, would become Elsie's favourite cousin.

James Lyle Mackay was raised to the peerage as Baron Inchcape of Strathnaver in 1911, advanced to viscount in 1924 and to the earldom in 1929, the year following his daughter's tragic flight. But one great honour that he declined was the request for him to join the monarchy by becoming the King of Albania. In a scene that would not have looked out of place in a Marx Brothers film, the serious offer of the throne of Albania was made when

Glenapp Castle, Ballantrae - The Mackay family estate in south-west Scotland.
(photograph courtesty of William Barraclough)

a special messenger arrived at Glenapp Castle, Mackay's Ayrshire home in south-west Scotland. The Baron was at lunch with the family at the time and the request was initially treated by everyone at the table as one of his pranks but the official missive, written on behalf of the Albanian Foreign Minister and influential government deputies, offered Lord Inchcape 'palaces in Tirana and Valona'. He replied with brevity: 'It is a great compliment to be offered the Crown of Albania but it is not in my line!'

The instructions left in Lord Inchcape's will further illustrate that, although he had gained great power, prestige and influence during his life, he never lost sight of his relatively humble background. Among his bequests were a year's wages to all the indoor and outdoor servants who had been in his employ for more than a year; £5000 each to his many nephews and nieces, a considerable sum in 1932; £1000 each to named staff at the British India S N Company and P&O; and annuities to household, personal and estate employees and staff at his firms in London, Glasgow and various places abroad. In one of the last provisions of his will Lord Inchcape declared himself a domiciled Scotsman and stated that it was his desire that his trust would be administered according to the law of Scotland. It stated that 'any attempt on the part of any of the beneficiaries to have the estate administered by the Courts of England or any other country shall be the occasion and ground of a forfeiture of beneficial rights.'

There is no doubt that his talent as a businessman was equal to his devotion to his family. One of his daughters recalled that if any of the children paid a visit to his study they were not admonished with orders not to touch anything – instead he had a special drawer in his desk where they were allowed to rummage to their hearts' content. Inchcape had a sense of humour that made him an entertaining playmate for any child in the family. Once, at the age of sixty, he was discovered trying to do an impromptu performance of circus-style balancing tricks using two chairs.

Although those who came across him in business or government circles thought of him as a hard man, he had the capacity for great kindness and spontaneous generosity, especially to those less fortunate than himself. In his later years he spent more and more time at sea, often fishing in Loch Ryan, the sea loch near Stranraer in south-west Scotland, just a few miles south of his Ayrshire estate. On one occasion he landed at the small harbour of Cairnryan, now the base for the P&O ferry service to Ireland, with a record catch of more than six hundred mackerel. As there was a large house party staying at Glenapp at the time, he had been told by Lady Inchcape that any fish caught would be a welcome addition to the larder. But, during the five-mile journey home, he stopped at almost every cottage to give away some of the fish and arrived back at the castle with only twelve mackerel left for his guests.

Elsie inherited many of her father's characteristics, drive and personality traits, perhaps more so than any of her siblings. This led her to be wilful and independent but also hugely popular amongst friends, colleagues, staff and the people of Ballantrae, the tiny village that nestles below the Glenapp estate. The boundless energy and wildness that so many teachers saw in the young

James Mackay could also be found in his favourite daughter – but it was these qualities that the father and daughter shared that would also cause them to clash, most spectacularly over Elsie's choice of husband and later her desire to fly the Atlantic.

Lord Inchcape had no such difficulties with his other children. His eldest son, the Honourable Kenneth Mackay, joined his father's business and become Viscount Glenapp and eventually the Second Earl of Inchcape. Lady Margaret Cargill Mackay married the Honourable Alexander Shaw, later the Second Baron Craigmyle and Liberal Member of Parliament for Kilmarnock before following his father-in-law into the chairmanship of P&O. Lady Janet Lyle Mackay married the eminent soldier Lieutenant-Colonel Frederick Bailey and Elsie's youngest sister, Effie, married the distinguished career diplomat Sir Eugene Millington-Drake.

Elsie also married but, like the rest of her choices in life, the man she fell in love with couldn't have been further from the ideal her parents would have wished for her. He was certainly completely unlike the peer, soldier and diplomat chosen by her sisters. Whatever was expected of a young woman in her position in society, Elsie knew her own mind and very determinedly followed her own path, although this ultimately proved to be in a direction with a mysterious destiny.

CHAPTER TWO

A Thirst for Adventure

Described as 'England's most glamorous aviatrix', the Honourable Elsie Mackay blazed a trail through 1920s' high society. Her attempt to fly the Atlantic was quite in character for a young woman who had already made a name for herself in a number of different fields whilst also straining the patience of her parents. 'Every luxury money commands has not satisfied Lord Inchcape's daughter in her thirst for adventure', blared *The New York Times* in March 1928 when the news of Elsie's flight hit the headlines. 'It is said that she is very wealthy in her own right. Her silver Rolls-Royce is the envy of motorists here; her gowns and jewels are the envy of many women.' But Elsie was not the flighty heiress depicted in many later articles by journalists and aviation writers. She was passionate rather than carelessly capricious, single-minded rather than selfish. She was described in one newspaper profile as 'exemplifying the phenomenon of the "New Woman" in post-war Britain.' She had inherited the same drive and determination that had seen her father rise from a 'humble box-wallah' to the peerage but, as a young woman in the 1920s even with her wealth and connections, opportunities to express these talents were limited.

There is no doubt that Elsie's young life was one of wealth and privilege. She was born in Simla, India, in 1893 but the family returned to Britain when she was still a baby. The Mackays established a home in London at Seamore Place in Mayfair and another in Scotland, initially in the north east. The 1901 census recorded the family, including seven-year-old Elsie, at Cairness House in Aberdeenshire with a household staff of fourteen servants. Despite the grandness of the family's lifestyle, there is no doubt that her parents were warm and loving to their children and later their grandchildren; Lord Inchcape was addressed as 'fatherman'. One of Elsie's sisters told Lord Inchcape's biographer Hector Bolitho that their father: 'never bullied us. One word of praise from him was worth the world to us. When we were children he taught us to ride and then to jump on our ponies. When we were naughty it was a terrible punishment to be sent for into father's study. He would give us a very stiff lecture. I remember one time in particular when he reduced me to tears. As I was leaving his study he called me back and said: "I know you are sorry and are going to try now and remember, Mousie mine, that your old father is always your friend."'

Elsie Mackay.
(photograph courtesty of William Barraclough)

Family friend Sir Thomas Catto once remarked on the similarity between Lord Inchcape and Elsie. 'He had unbounded pride and affection for her. She was undoubtedly remarkable and had inherited much of his force and personality.' Although the family's wealth and position would have enabled Elsie to live a life of luxury and ease, she had clearly inherited her father's determination and dynamism and she was not content with the sometimes hedonistic social whirl of many aristocratic 'bright young things' of her generation. This was a time of great social change that saw dramatic strides in the role of women in society. In the twenties a phenomenon referred to as the 'Modern Girl' or the 'Modern Young Woman' had its origins in the suffragettes and the wave of female emancipation brought on by the numbers of women who had been encouraged to join the Volunteer Aid Detachment during the Great War.

Like many young women, Elsie had wanted to do her bit for the war effort when the conflict in Europe started in August 1914. Her desire to help was prompted not only by the general wave of volunteering that swept through the population but also because she had received her education at a convent school in Belgium, the country that had taken the brunt of the initial German attack on the outbreak of hostilities; she was doubtless distressed by what might have happened to her teachers and schoolmates.

The call for nurses in the early years of the war was answered by women from a variety of backgrounds including, according to historian Yvonne McEwen: 'the society darlings who had tangoed away the hours in plush hotels and posh parlours and who now discovered they could have a more "meaningful" way of occupying their time.' In her book *It's a Long Way to Tipperary, British and Irish Nurses in the Great War* she quotes a socialite from Surrey who epitomised the background of many of the women who volunteered for the nursing services: 'It was an absolutely wonderful life, all parties, all fun, all dances … we really had a gay life … everyone did. There was a sort of an idea of war and people began thinking, should we do something?'

When Lady Inchcape opened a hospital for officers at their London home in Seamore Place, Elsie and her sisters immediately volunteered to nurse shoulder to shoulder with other young women. In such mixed company society girls often picked up habits like smoking 'gaspers' and learning army slang but there was even more in store for the Inchcapes – Elsie also picked up a husband. A young South African actor serving with the Wiltshire Regiment was sent to the hospital to recuperate from injuries sustained in a poison gas attack and a serious fall whilst serving on the Western Front in France. Tall, fair and handsome, Dennis Wyndham was the son of Major William Wyndham of the 45th Regiment of Sherwood Foresters and his wife Julia. The dashing thirty year old had a colourful career history before joining the army, having worked as a mounted police officer in Natal, a cow puncher, heavyweight boxer, sailor and a miner before gaining some acting experience on stage in Johannesburg. He made his debut on the London stage as part of Sir Herbert Tree's company in 1911 and appeared with the famous actress Mrs Patrick Campbell.

✦

The couple met in the romantic circumstances of being nurse and patient. Although twenty-three-year-old Elsie was certainly smitten, her father was not taken with Dennis, just as he had been unimpressed with his sister's choice many years before. He did not believe that the young officer was suitable material to be his son-in-law. In November 1916, when Elsie informed Lord Inchcape that she wished to marry Dennis Wyndham, he 'expressed strong dissent against the marriage.' When the lieutenant formally asked Lord Inchcape for Elsie's hand he was refused permission on the grounds that he had been on the stage. The strength of Lord Inchcape's opposition to the match was met with an equal amount of emotion from his daughter, who became quite ill during the winter of 1916. Whether it was heartache, disappointment, exhaustion from her nursing experiences or a combination of them all, Elsie fled to their Scottish home at Glenapp to rest, giving her time to nurse her broken heart – and hatch a plan.

Separation only made the attachment between Elsie and her young South African suitor all the stronger. In the spring of 1917 she was no less determined to make this man her husband and the couple became secretly engaged, despite rumours circulating that she had been threatened with disinheritance by her father if she went ahead with the relationship. Knowing that during the month of May her parents would be travelling north to Glenapp for a few weeks at the Ayrshire estate, she set her plan to elope with Dennis into action.

Lord Inchcape had made discreet inquiries into Wyndham's background when his daughter became besotted with the wounded soldier and it was, perhaps, through these same agents that he received information that made him very suspicious about Elsie's activities. He returned unexpectedly to the Mayfair house on May 19th. Elsie and Dennis, believing their intentions remained a secret, kept their appointment with a London registrar – only to be met by a solicitor sent by Lord Inchcape, who had caught wind of their marriage plan. The agent raised objections to their wedding and prevented the ceremony from going ahead. But the drama was only just beginning and what followed was a breathless dash around London that would not have been out of place in a screwball comedy or an early Hitchcock thriller.

Dennis had been on a period of leave from his regiment due to his injuries but this had now expired. With their wedding plan foiled, the young couple made to leave the registrar's office only to discover that someone had tipped off the provost marshals that the lieutenant was absent without leave from his regiment; they were waiting outside ready to haul the officer back to barracks to face charges.

Elsie realised that the marshals were probably on the lookout not only at the registrar's but also at Wyndham's lodgings in Pall Mall. The couple managed somehow to slip out of the registrar's office unseen and made a dash into a nearby restaurant. Here Elsie explained how they were a young couple in love, desperate to marry but their wedding had been prevented by the intervention of her father and she begged the staff to help them escape. Swept up by the romance of the adventure, and aided no doubt by Dennis's skills as an actor, the sympathetic restaurant staff supplied a change of clothes to help with their disguise, enabling Dennis to get out of his army uniform. A taxi was hailed and the couple were smuggled out of the restaurant. Keen to steer clear of any police who might have been alerted to their escape, they avoided the main railway stations and were driven instead to London's Willesden Junction, where they boarded a train heading north. Elsie had come up with a new plan – they would elope to Scotland.

Actor Dennis Wyndham eloped to Scotland with Elsie Mackay - pursued by Lord Inchape's agents. *(Image courtesy of The National Portrait Gallery, William Hustler and Georgina Hustler)*

In a further attempt to elude any pursuers, Elsie and Dennis travelled to Glasgow in a third-class carriage filled with sailors and soldiers going home on leave from the war. Arriving in Glasgow, the couple stayed with friends of the lieutenant's and hurriedly organised a wedding.

They were married at the Catholic church of St Aloysius in the centre of the Scottish city, just a stone's throw from bustling Sauchiehall Street, on May 23rd 1917. Although Dennis stated that his home was in Piccadilly, London,

Elsie gave her address as 8 Hill Street, Glasgow, just a five-minute walk from the church. She also described her father as being James Mackay, a shipping contractor, rather than Lord Inchcape, chairman of P&O. The American magazine *Time* described Elsie as being 'unimpressed by her father's millions', claiming that she had laughed at the threat of disinheritance.

They returned to London on the night train but the newly-wed runaways' euphoria evaporated at the sobering sight of the provost marshal who was there to meet them at Euston station. Although the soldier arrested Elsie's new husband for desertion, the blushing bride must have worked her considerable charm on the arresting officer. "The provost marshal was a splendid fellow," Lieutenant Wyndham told the newspapers. "He took us to his house and gave us a splendid breakfast." He also reunited Dennis with the uniform he had cast off at the restaurant.

When he was tried before a general, the lieutenant got away with a 'suitable wigging, there was no bitterness in the reprimand. The general seemed to be smiling,' according to the columnist in the Australian newspaper *The New South Wales Leader*. Dennis certainly seemed to get off very lightly as he was promoted to captain before being invalided out of the army later the same year. It is impossible not to see the powerful influence of Lord Inchcape somewhere in the background of the leniency and promotion shown to the unexpected son-in-law.

It appears that Elsie wasn't quite ready to settle down to married life though, or perhaps the excitement of the elopement didn't turn into the enduring romance she'd been expecting. For a short period at the end of 1918 she volunteered as a 'dashing car driver' attached to a training regiment of the Royal Air Force at Northolt and the 'sight of her big Crossley burning up the Uxbridge road with a load of brass-hats was a common sight,' according to one Australian newspaper. *The Richmond River Herald* wrote that 'speed records led the Hon Elsie Mackay to be reduced to a Ford. Even on this she managed to keep the Ruislip road relatively free of unwary pedestrians, and later on was further reduced to a lowly Douglas motorcycle.'

As a new decade arrived, like many women who had enjoyed the freedoms and opportunities that had been extended to them by the demands of the war effort, Elsie found it difficult to settle to life as the wife of a struggling actor. Many young people, especially those in high society circles, reacted to the post-war period by throwing themselves into a round of hedonistic party going. Dancing all night at The Ritz, treasure hunts, practical jokes and fancy-dress parties all contributed to the early 1920s being given the title 'Roaring'. This change amongst those who had survived or served through the horrors of the First World War was a combination of grief, relief and the resulting social upheaval. The post-war period saw, perhaps for the first time, the rebellion of youth so familiar to parents today. One of the famous Mitford girls later recalled that the 1920s was like an ongoing guerrilla war at home, with arguments between her parents and her sisters over lipstick, smoking, wearing trousers and the new short 'shingled' hairstyle.

The antics of these young people from the middle and upper classes featured frequently in newspaper columns, entrancing readers with their escapades. People became famous simply due to their repeated appearances in the pages of *The Daily Express* and *The Daily Mail*. Press baron Lord Northcliffe, owner of *The Daily Mail*, was keen to feature these society snippets believing they sold papers; he told his editor that he wanted 'more names in the paper, the more aristocratic the better.' Through the prism of the press, the social life of London's young and privileged appeared to be one long, boisterous, cocktail-fuelled party.

Elsie Mackay was certainly a 'name' and a dazzling presence in society, often appearing in the diary columns of the well connected. 'Dark, not unattractive, graceful, habitually well-gowned and bejewelled, Miss Mackay was the envy of women. Her silver Rolls-Royce flashed at breakneck speed. Her horses invariably galloped,' *Time* magazine told its readers. *The Manchester Guardian* society columnist remarked that 'she is very good-looking and considered one of the best-dressed women and dancers in London society.'

The term 'flapper' was coined during this period, a word used to describe the new freedom of the raised hem and the dropped waist of modern fashion, the less constricted style of the modern girl, although later it would be used to imply an empty-headed silliness and thoughtless gaiety. Although Elsie could have easily fallen into this merry-go-round of Mayfair society, characterised by its extravagance, whimsicality and excess, she was instead 'quite one of the most remarkable women of the younger generation although her modesty has prevented the public from hearing much of her exploits', according to one society columnist.

One of these first post-war exploits came about due to the connections of her husband, who had returned to acting at the end of the war. She found fame on the silver screen as the cinema actress 'Poppy Wyndham'. The adoption of the new name may have been, to some degree, an attempt to protect her family from the embarrassment of having a daughter taking part in this new phenomenon initially known as the 'kinema'. However, it may also have been due to the fact that there was an Australian actress called Elsie Mackay who had already established a career in her home country before appearing on the London stage and later on Broadway in New York. She married the famous leading man Lionel Atwill but the marriage ended in scandal when it was discovered that she was having an affair with the actor Max Montesole. Due to errors in the media as early as 1928, which continue to be compounded today by the internet, the careers of the two women are often mistakenly mixed up. The Honourable Elsie Mackay never acted under her own name and only ever performed as a cinema actress.

Although it was very unusual for someone of Elsie's background, she was not unique in her move to become an actress on the silver screen. In an article entitled 'The New Profession', a writer with *The Derby Daily Telegraph* described how film acting had: 'an extraordinary fascination for many young fellows. There is nothing infra dig about it for recruits are being drawn from the ranks of our leading actors and actresses but also from the peerage.' A millionaire's son called Eric Gordon had apparently abandoned the diplomatic service for film production; others tempted by the studio lights included Lady Doris Stapleton, Sir Simeon Stuart and, of course, Poppy Wyndham. The journalist explained the possible attraction: 'film acting does not involve the wearisome repetition inevitable in ordinary theatrical life. Not only are there adventures and variety in it, but there is also a good deal of money.' It was therefore perfect for Elsie, a woman drawn to adventure and, if the rumours were true about her disinheritance, perhaps also in need of an income.

Elsie under her screen name - Poppy Wyndham.
(photograph author's own)

As Poppy Wyndham, Elsie enjoyed a brief but successful career, starring in a number of silent movies made by one of the most important studios of the period, the Broadwest Film Company. The studio, founded by director Walter

West and George Broadbridge (later Lord Broadbridge), produced films shot in a huge glass studio in Walthamstow, east London. Films made by Broadwest were not only released in Britain but also exported to countries in Europe and all over the world, including India, New Zealand, Scandinavia and the USA. Although Elsie began with 'crowd work', she became a named cast member in movies like *Snow in the Desert* and *A Great Coup*, both made in 1919; she soon became the leading lady in other films including *A Dead Certainty* and *Tidal Wave*, in which she played a young artist rescued from drowning by a fisherman with whom she subsequently has a romance. Elsie often played opposite established actors who, in some cases, went on to enjoy careers in Hollywood such as the British star Ronald Colman, who later appeared in films like *Bulldog Drummond* and *Lost Horizon*.

As Poppy, Elsie was certainly a versatile actress and appeared in movies ranging from comedies to romantic melodramas. In 1920 a *Times* film critic noted that *A Dead Certainty*, a picture set in the field of horse racing, featured 'some good acting by Miss Poppy Wyndham' and showcased some of her many talents. Film goers were told that the story included 'novel outdoor stunts. Miss Wyndham is one of the very few stars who can ride a horse at breakneck speed.' She was also described as 'performing a series of hair raising stunts with the utmost nonchalance and success.'

Elsie narrowly escaped being burned to death during the filming for her role in *The Great Coup*. In December 1919 one newspaper reported that she was perched on a chair arm near a fire when the fringe of her dress caught light and quickly went up in flames. 'Her husband, who was luckily in the room at the time, rushed for an overcoat and rolling his terrified wife up in the coat soon extinguished the flames but not before he had received severe burns on his arms and hands. Luckily Miss Wyndham had been able to continue her work.'

In *Son of David*, filmed in 1920, Poppy played opposite leading man Ronald Colman for a second time, on this occasion taking the part of Esther Raphael, the daughter of a rabbi in a gritty drama about the world of boxing. Although in 1918 Broadwest was recognised as one of the most important studios in Britain, the post-war boom was short-lived and by 1921, along with a number of other production companies, it ran into financial difficulties and went into liquidation. Sadly, many of these films from the early days of British cinema were lost in the London Blitz during the Second World War. All that's left from this period of Elsie's cinema career is the publicity shot of her posing in a striped dress smiling at the camera.

One fact that is true about the actress Elsie Mackay and Elsie under her Poppy Wyndham persona is that their marriages both ended in scandal. Elsie was not involved in an affair like her Australian namesake, but the very fact that her marriage ended was scandalous enough for her family and the society circles they moved in. Her brief marriage to Dennis Wyndham ended with an annulment in February 1922, thereby managing to avert the further social stigma of a divorce but still causing 'something of a sensation'.

Whatever the real unhappiness behind the breakdown of her marriage, Elsie was able to end their relationship due to a technicality when the case came before Lord Anderson in the Edinburgh courts. Elsie's legal team argued that her marriage contract was null and void as she had not been resident in Scotland for the required fifteen days before the wedding. As the runaway couple only arrived in the country on the 19th or 20th of May and married on the 23rd, she had not even been in Scotland for five days. Elsie had signed various forms indicating that she had been resident in Scotland for the required period but in court she claimed that she had only glanced at the details due to her excitement at the prospect of her impending marriage. Her father's appearance at the hearing on his daughter's behalf may also have influenced the judge's somewhat compassionate decision. Elsie left court scot free whilst other bit players in the drama, the Glaswegians who had witnessed Elsie's signature, received a severe admonishment from the judge.

It is not clear whether Elsie was ever formally disinherited during the period of her marriage and estranged from her family because of her impulsive attachment to Dennis Wyndham, but her father's appearance in the Edinburgh divorce court indicates that by this point all was forgiven between them. Elsie left behind her husband and her brief flirtation with the glamour of the cinema and returned to life with her family at Seamore Place and her beloved Glenapp Castle.

Elsie at Carlock House on the Glenapp Estate with
her sister, Margaret.
(photograph courtesy of William Barraclough)

In July 1922, *The Times* newspaper in London reported that Elsie had
resumed her maiden name of Mackay, a name that would appear frequently
again in the society columns. A *Times* report in July the following year is
typical, describing a dance given in London for Elsie by her mother Lady
Inchcape. Elsie wore a 'Victorian picture dress of pink and gold brocade
over an underskirt of silver lace.' The austerity many suffered in the post-
war period clearly did not apply to the lifestyle of the Inchcapes. The report
continued: 'The ballroom comprised three communicating reception rooms
decorated with pink roses and white lilies. The veranda, which was used for
sitting, was decorated with palms, the supper room with yellow roses and the
staircase and landing with mauve rhododendrons and white lilies. Music was
by the Ambrose Band.' The list of guests reads like a who's who of high society
and included the ambassadors of France and Belgium, along with the Earl of
Galloway, the Duchess of Somerset and Prince Paul of Serbia.

Although such events were an indication that all was forgiven at home, Elsie
remained restless for a life beyond the social whirl of parties, balls, lunches and
charity work. Alert for an opportunity for further adventure, Elsie's interest
was piqued by the attractions of travel in the form of flying and her father's
business – shipping. It is entirely possible, and it would have been quite in
character, for Elsie to have become enamoured with aviation during her brief

period as a driver for the 'brass-hats' of the Royal Air Force at the end of the war. It is highly likely that she would have used her charm to persuade a young pilot to take her up in one of the biplanes during her stint as a volunteer. At the end of her marriage she lost no time in getting herself back up into the sky.

Aviation was still in its infancy; the Wright Brothers had made that first brief flight in a heavier-than-air contraption only twenty years before. These were heady days for those able to take part either in the growing air industry or those wealthy enough to take up flying as an exhilarating and dangerous hobby. It says something about Lord Inchcape's indulgence for his wayward daughter that he did not try to prevent her taking up flying even though he disliked the new phenomenon intensely and never went in an aircraft in all his life. *The New York Times* described Elsie as being 'steel nerved, whether astride a horse, guiding an airplane or being "shot" in a London studio.' She certainly needed those nerves of steel during her first flying lesson. 'The marvel is that she has never broken her neck,' one of her first tutors, Captain E. C. D. Herne, said at the time.

His description of one their first flights together is certainly hair-raising. While at something over 10,000 feet Elsie shouted to Captain Herne that he should loop the plane round the other way, meaning that the manoeuvre should be made with the wheels of the landing carriage on the inside of the circle. The captain knew that this would put a terrific strain on every strut and wire in the reverse direction to which they were designed to withstand; nevertheless he pushed the nose of the machine down and turned her over. Later, relating the incident to newspaper reporters, the pilot said that the 'wind had shrieked in their ears' and he saw the wings fluttering under the strain like 'a flag in a gale'. But worse was to come: Elsie's safety strap broke but she managed to catch and grip the bracing wires, holding on for grim death while her body swung outside the plane 'like a stone twirled on the end of a piece of string.' When Captain Herne returned the plane to the ground with difficulty, he discovered that Elsie's hands had been cut to the bone due to her fearsome grip of the wires. Yet, he told reporters, her response to his concern had been that 'she was ready to repeat the exploit any time – as long as she was given a stronger safety belt.'

Elsie went on to receive lessons from one of the leading pilots of the day, Sir Alan Cobham, who flew out of the Stag Lane aerodrome in Hendon. He had such confidence in her ability as an airwoman that he allowed her to fly several of the biggest machines that they had there. On August 14th 1922, the Honourable Elsie Mackay obtained her flying certificate, number 7930, from the Royal Aero Club – one of the earliest British women to secure it. With further training at the de Havilland school in Edgware, Elsie's success followed shortly after a Mrs Atkey, who was believed to have been the first woman to learn to fly in the post-war period.

One of the tests pilots had to complete to gain a flying licence was to ascend to a height of 5000 feet alone and make three perfect landings. The planes in which these tests were taken were not machines with big safety factors but 360-horse-power de Havilland-6 biplanes, a plane that had been used routinely as a training machine by the Royal Flying Corps during the war.

In 1925 Elsie's experience as an aviator was such that she was elected to become a member of the advisory committee of pilots to the British Empire Air League. The following year *The Times* reported that Elsie gave a lunch with her father for guests, including Sir Alan and Lady Cobham, and Air Vice Marshall Sir Sefton Brancker, who would play a vital part in Elsie's Atlantic attempt and who later lost his life in the R101 airship disaster. Also present at the lunch was a Miss Sophie Ries, a close friend of Elsie's, who would become one of the small circle who knew of her secret plans to conquer the Atlantic.

At the end of her marriage Elsie began to spend more time with the family either at the Mayfair town house or the estate at Glenapp. For a short time the Inchcapes owned Chesterford Park on the border between Cambridgeshire and Essex but in 1917 the mansion was sold so that the family could, once again, return home to Scotland whenever possible.

Glenapp Castle was built in the Scottish baronial style in 1870 by David Bryce for James Hunter, who was then the deputy Lord Lieutenant of Ayrshire. Surrounded by 15,000 acres, Lord Inchcape was able to take pleasure in two of his favourite pastimes – shooting game over the estate's moorland and sailing from nearby Loch Ryan in his yacht. He added a beautiful room to the castle by creating two great windows: one that looked up a slope of lawn to rhododendrons and dark firs, and the other that framed his favourite vista looking out towards the sea beyond the small village of Ballantrae with an almost perfect view of the distinctly shaped small island of Ailsa Craig. With the creation of this room, which would be his escape from the bustle of guests and family, he took an interest in interior design, even taking shopping trips with his wife to buy a desk, table and chairs. Two vast silver sailing ships were placed in each window and his desk in the centre of the room. To the delight of his grandchildren, he also kept a beautiful French musical box in gold and turquoise enamel. If a child visited his study, he would open the box to reveal a tiny bird made from real feathers that would rise up from a gilded net to greet them with a song.

When Lord Inchcape served on the Geddes committee, an influential post-war government think-tank, the businessmen who made up the group – known as the 'Big Five' – met at Glenapp to work out the detailed recommendations they later presented to Parliament. The Mackay family's growing fortunes can be seen from the increase in servants and staff, from fourteen recorded in the Aberdeenshire house in the 1901 census to more than eighty-eight employed in the house, gardens and forests of Glenapp, with a further thirty crew aboard the yacht, *The Rover*.

The relative remoteness of Glenapp Castle must have provided a welcome bolthole for twenty-eight-year-old Elsie when she needed to escape the attentions of the society press, especially during the sensation that marked the end of her marriage. For all her dynamism and steely nerve Elsie, like her father, had a sensitive and caring nature that was well known to the staff at the south Ayrshire estate. The Ballantrae correspondent of the local paper, *The Girvan Town Crier and Pavilion News*, recorded that: 'Miss Mackay is a favourite in the village. We have evidence of her skill as an airwoman as for some time she was a constant flyer in her own machine in and around the district. Intrepid rather than daring describes the petite lady who numbers every inhabitant here her friend. Her great interest in the children, in the

British Legion and all things pertaining to the welfare of her less fortunate neighbours endeared her to all hearts. She was most approachable, and as a well-known resident described her, was free from wealth consciousness. She is at home in the air, at the wheel of a car, on the stage, at a simple country festival or taking part in a Royal function.'

In an article that appeared in the local paper, *The Stranraer Advertiser and Free Press*, another village reporter wrote of the great kindness and energy of the woman everyone knew locally as 'Miss Elsie': 'She would undertake an all-night motor run from London to Glenapp where she would arrive as a winter morn was breaking and then hasten to the public hall to prepare for a concert and a dance to be held in the evening on behalf of a public cause. The concert over – and to a great extent it would be the creation of herself – she would mingle with the dancers and dance for hours with manifest joy.'

Miss Elsie had a reputation for her generosity and gaiety. At Christmas, in particular, she was said to be like a child again playing with the village children and often lavishly entertaining them and showering them with expensive presents. These festive parties would be recalled by those children in much later life, remaining as cherished memories, and many continued to treasure the china dolls they had been given by Miss Elsie.

As a frequent visitor at the village tearoom situated in the main street next to McCreath's bakery, Elsie got to know the young girls who worked there. One, a young woman called Mary Davidson, was a fine soprano singer who regularly took part in local concerts with her sister Jenny. Elsie was so impressed with the girl's natural talent that she made arrangements for her to travel to Italy to train as an opera singer. Unfortunately, as later recalled by Jenny's daughter Janette McCulloch, Mary was not allowed to take up this extraordinary opportunity because their mother didn't feel she could be spared from the family business.

Such gestures were typical of Elsie. Another that featured in many newspaper reports at the time of the Atlantic attempt involved one of the young gardeners at Glenapp who had completed his apprenticeship. Just before he was leaving for an appointment, Elsie presented him with a pound note and a handsome wrist watch before sending him off to the railway station in her own car.

Lady Inchcape was often glad of Elsie's helpful presence at Glenapp; when her own health failed her daughter took over the arrangements for entertaining house guests or visiting dignitaries. But life wasn't all kindness and duty. Elsie flew her plane, galloped across the moors on her horse and there were stories of wild parties at a small beach house in a secluded bay on the estate when Elsie would reportedly negotiate the rocky winding track to the sea in her Rolls Royce.

Spending more time with her family brought Elsie under the steady influence of her father, a man who kept a strict and regular routine. It was through him that she gained a new opportunity to channel her extraordinary drive and energy that would never have been satisfied just by the domestic role of helping her mother at home. Elsie began to work as a designer for P&O, the company her father had helped to create and of which he was, by then, chairman. Although there may have been many who believed this appointment was simply an act of nepotism, others argued that Lord Inchcape was too shrewd a businessman to risk giving a high-profile job to his daughter if he didn't believe she was capable of doing it.

In 1926, P&O had reported a net loss of more than £300,000 and Lord Inchcape had issued a directive saying that he 'saw it as imperative that the P&O standards especially in the luxury liner business should be as high as possible', according to Stephanie Jones, author of *Trade and Shipping: Lord Inchcape 1852–1932*. The change in economic fortunes for many countries in the fallout following the First World War led to something of a crisis in shipping. The war had opened up the market and several countries, including America and Italy, were vying for position in the area of luxury ocean travel. According to author Anne Wealleans, author of *Designing Liners: A History of Interior Design Afloat*: 'many of the key ocean liner interiors of the interwar years were examples of the national showcase, framing what was considered the best design style and the best designers by the liners owners.' These new countries competing with the old shipping companies used indigenous designers to 'express a more contemporary style in the service of national identity.'

Taking up her position as artistic director, Elsie was responsible for cabin decorations and kitchen arrangements, initially on the steamers trading with the East and later on the new Australian fleet. Her appointment caused some consternation among the older captains and officers of this famous shipping line but she proved her worth. As in aviation, Elsie was once again leading the way for women. According to Anne Wealleans: 'she was one of the first examples of a woman working on ship interiors though she was largely unacknowledged at the time.'

Although P&O still used professional decorating firms, Elsie was responsible for the interiors of the new ship the *Viceroy of India*. This was a vessel of great significance for the company. At 19,648 gross tons it was the largest ever built for P&O and it was designed to rescue their failing fortunes. Featuring luxury interiors and technical innovations, it was the first European-owned turbo-electric ship, which was seen as an 'epoch-making event in the annals of British shipbuilding' according to one of *Shipbuilder* magazine's commentators at the time. In April 1925 the board of P&O agreed that Elsie would be awarded £600 a quarter as an adviser on the interior décor of its ships and the *Viceroy of India* in particular. By then Elsie and her mother had travelled frequently with Lord Inchcape and developed opinions on the state of ship interiors, particularly the lack of modern amenities. Together they had advised on the public rooms for the vessel *Raznak*, introduced in February 1925 for the Aden to Bombay route.

Lord Inchcape, though obviously confident in his daughter's abilities, remained sensitive about the appointment and he secretly arranged for her salary to be paid from his own 'emoluments'. His greatest concern, though, appears to have been about Elsie's modern ideas. Contemporary reviews expressed anxiety about the 'distinctive modern note' of the décor. Decorating companies working on British ships during this period tended to stick to a more traditional style and Elsie ruffled a few feathers with her ideas. Despite being a product of the Victorian age, Lord Inchcape was a successful businessman who recognised the need to move with the times. He was quoted as commenting, perhaps a little defensively: 'I feel some diffidence on assenting to my daughter being given this appointment but I conscientiously believe it will be a good thing for the P&O company – we are building ships which, unless they come to grief, will be on the service for the next twenty years and we have to look ahead.'

And look ahead Elsie certainly did. Working in conjunction with the distinguished London decorators Waring and Gillow, she devised 'refreshing and harmonious colour schemes in which every detail, from curtains and carpets to style of furniture and upholstery, is fitted into the concept' according to one Australian reporter. She brought with her the taste of the British upper class but combined it with a touch of the glamorous world of movie-making, taking her lead from new innovations introduced on the transatlantic routes.

The *Viceroy of India* was the first P&O ship to have a swimming pool. The smoking room, although designed by a woman, was exclusively used by men and was modelled on an early-seventeenth-century palace built for James I of England, James VI of Scotland. The music room blended classical styles with a distinctive modern note, the light fittings were art deco and she introduced new innovations to the first-class 'cabines-de-luxe' in that for the first time they had private bathrooms, a wardrobe, washbasin with running water, book rack, coffee tray and the novelty of a reading lamp. The rooms were panelled in polished hardwood and featured art deco wood inlay on the walls.

Excitement about Elsie's new designs was reported around the British Empire. In May 1925 *The Australasian* carried news of her work on a new fifteen-thousand-ton liner, the *Cathay*, which had left on its maiden voyage. 'The public rooms and staterooms should be, as far as possible, like their homes ashore. There should be plenty of cushions, bright covers and footstools,' Elsie announced at the ship's launch. British newspaper reporters were very taken with the 'green Jacobean smoke-room and Adams music room.' *The Manchester Guardian's* society columnist commented: 'In all the dozen ships which she has redecorated Miss Mackay has adopted modern ideas of decoration with gay, cheerful paint and panelling on the walls, plenty of prints and etchings and cheerful silk hangings.'

Not everyone was taken with Elsie's new designs. She'd chosen mauve carpets and furnishings together with satinwood furniture for the rooms occupied by Lord and Lady Reading on their return journey to India. One newspaper reported that an old skipper 'nearly had apoplexy on seeing the accommodation provided in the ship.' Elsie told journalists at the launch of the *Cathay* that her footstools had brought her into conflict with the vessel's captain, whom she described as an 'old fashioned salt'. Captain Bartlett informed her that he liked a 'ship-shape' vessel and had no use for silk cushions and libraries with up-to-date novels; '…such "fal-lals" were all very well for a yacht, but not for a liner,' he told Miss Mackay. 'I have been 43 years at sea and in my early days we were thankful for ship's biscuits and pea soup and ate off our sea chests.' Elsie retorted that: 'if he really believed in the good old days he should give up his cabin and his bath and go back to his biscuit served on a camp stool.'

Joining P&O had further revealed just how alike Lord Inchcape and his daughter were in character. One feature writer in *The Daily Express* commented: 'I have never known a woman so full of vitality. When she was engaged in decorating her father's P&O liners she frequently arrived to begin work at 6 o'clock in the morning – and Heaven help the members of staff who were not equally early.'

Friends described Elsie as 'always busy'; 'I must always be doing something' was her frequent remark. Elsie thought nothing of flying to Scotland for the weekend to see her parents, or over to Paris for a few days, but she was very serious about her work for P&O. She created an office in the top floor of Seamore Place described by one commentator in 1928 as 'like a man's, filled with files on shipping and other details in which she was interested.' The same writer added: 'despite her work she never neglected her appearance and was one of the best-dressed women in London. Her strength, determination and ability to carry out her plans were almost masculine, but she was essentially womanly, sensitive and sympathetic. She loved children and animals, her constant companions were a mongrel and an aged pug dog known as Rumple.'

Not only was Elsie in charge of artistic design, she was also like a super housekeeper to the shipping line. Immediately one of the ships docked in London after a voyage, she would make a full inspection of all the household arrangements and decorations, deciding what repairs were necessary and arranging for the work to be done. Writing in *The Catholic Press*, a 'friend' said: 'She never takes any breakfast, but has a cup of tea when she gets up. She then drives herself to the docks, where she has been known to arrive as early as six o'clock and remains there working hard all day. I have rung her up sometimes at 8.30 in the evening and found she was not yet back.'

The same writer described how she had first met Elsie Mackay in the early years of the war: 'I was ushered up a winding staircase of a huge London house into a palatial drawing-room overlooking the park. My hostess, a pretty brunette, was entertaining some young officers and friends and two daughters of the house – both small in stature and very dark – were helping to hand round tea. At a first glance these young girls looked almost like twins, but after a few minutes I realised that one was a plump and jolly schoolgirl while her sister at once impressed me as a girl of most unusual character. There was a determination about the elder girl's every action, a spirit of daring and adventure shone through her clear brown eyes, and her magnetic personality drew us all around her. We listened to her low, soft voice, which seemed almost to mesmerise us, as she told of little incidents connected with her hospital nursing or school adventures in the Belgian convent where she finished her education. This was my first meeting with the Hon. Elsie Mackay.'

Other writers commented on the contrast between her physique and her personality. One said: 'she is small – she barely reached to my shoulder but she has the heart of a lion.'

Elsie was so successful in her new career that she was personally responsible for the preparation of the apartments aboard the liner *Ranchi* that provided the accommodation for Princess Mary, the daughter of George V and sister of the future George VI, and her husband, Viscount Lascelles, on their voyage to Egypt in the spring of 1928. The work also proved to be the perfect decoy for her parents from the preparations she was secretly making behind the scenes. Representing the company and also as a friend of Princess Mary, Elsie was present at Victoria Station in London to 'bid adieu' to the royal party wearing a slim coat of a 'lovely bright blue shade that exactly matched her little felt hat'. Her attendance was also part of a deliberate smokescreen to prevent any suspicion falling on her real plans – to fly the Atlantic from east to west. Despite having nerves of steel there was just one thing she was afraid of – her father because he had the power to scupper her schemes. One *Daily Express* reporter later claimed that she had said: 'If you tell my father of my plans he will never forgive me.'

Glamorous even in her flying gear - the
Honourable Elsie Mackay.
(photograph courtesty of Laurie Notaro)

Despite the dreadful death toll already claimed by the depths of the Atlantic Ocean Elsie set the wheels in motion in 1927 for another attempt to make a crossing in a heavier-than-air craft. Her passion for flying combined her wilfulness and her thirst for adventure. Writing in 1936 about the milestones in aviation, Clifford W. Collinson and Captain F. McDermott said: 'Miss

Mackay was not a young and over-impulsive girl. She was over thirty years of age with a varied and interesting career behind her. But it was to flying that her heart was entirely given. She was, however, fully aware that her father would look with extreme disfavour on any such project and in consequence all preparations had to be made with the strictest secrecy.'

Due to her position in society and because of her vivacious and generous nature, Elsie Mackay was well connected and well liked. Working in utmost secrecy, she managed to persuade friends at the Air Ministry to recommend someone willing to risk flying the Atlantic east to west; the name they came up with was the famous pilot Captain W. G. R. Hinchliffe. As he was known to be against women flying she had somehow to persuade him to co-pilot a plane with her westward across the Atlantic.

CHAPTER THREE

A Wartime Ace and Career Pilot

The challenge of flying the Atlantic was first discussed by the Honourable Elsie Mackay and Captain Hinchliffe over lunch at The Ritz hotel in London in 1927. The man chosen by Elsie to help her achieve her ambition to become the first woman to fly the Atlantic was already famous – and not only amongst his fellow pilots. With over nine thousand flying hours, Captain Walter George Raymond Hinchliffe was one of the most accomplished airmen in the world. By the time he was introduced to Miss Mackay he was a settled family man, though his image belied a colourful past. It was this edge to his character, combined with superb flying skills, that made him the man most likely to conquer the treacherous east-to-west route. It was said of him that: 'an aeroplane, no matter of what type, is never safer than when in Capt. Hinchliffe's hands.'

Known as Ray or Hinch, he was born in Germany, the son of middle-class parents who originally hailed from Manchester. His father, Richard, was an artist, wealthy enough to be described in the 1901 census as 'living on private means'. By the time of this survey the family, comprising nine-year-old Raymond, his younger sister Gladys and parents Richard and Florence, had returned to England and set up home in Bedford Street, Liverpool. A young German woman travelled with them to work in the new household as a domestic servant.

This cosmopolitan background helps to explain the young Raymond's many and varied accomplishments. He could paint, speak four languages including German and French and was an avid reader. He was athletic – later described by *The New York Times* as a 'perfect physical specimen' – and had gained a number of sporting trophies during his youth, including the title of English middleweight amateur boxing champion. Hinch was also a good mechanic and in his youth had become fascinated by cars, speed and engines.

The subject of his date and place of birth illustrates what a colourful and interesting character Hinch was and raises the question of how much about him should be believed. According to his army papers, he was born on June 10th 1891, his navy record claims that it was 1893, the Royal Air Force states 1894 and court papers 1892. The 1901 census records that he was born in Germany, information that must have come from his father Richard as the head of the household and therefore should be reliable. Probably because of Germany having become the enemy during the First World War, Hinch's pilot's licence from the Royal Aero Club gives his birthplace as Liverpool with the date 'the 11th of June 1894', though the last digit has apparently been smudged and altered.

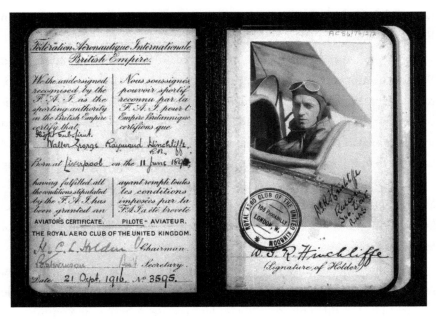

Image of Walter George Raymond Hinchliffe's pilot's licence.
(photograph courtesy of the Royal Aero Club Trust)

For a young man with a keen interest in engines, it was perhaps inevitable that Hinch would soon be caught up with the new and exciting world of aviation. He first took to the air in 1912, learning to fly at Brooklands aerodrome in Surrey. At this time he was flying for fun as before the war he had started to study medicine at Liverpool University, taking a course in dentistry as part of his studies. At other times, though, he described his pre-war occupation as 'artist'.

In 1912 Hinch joined the West Lancashire Territorial Army Service Corps and was commissioned as a second lieutenant. As a young man clearly still searching for a career path, he certainly found a sense of purpose in the air and he was able to put this talent to good use when war was declared in August 1914. The Territorials were en route to their annual camp when news of the war caused them to be diverted to make preparations for active service. The men who volunteered for service overseas were therefore amongst the first waves of the British Expeditionary Force sent across the channel, arriving in France in November 1914.

The West Lancashire Service Corps served in Rouen before returning to Weeton Camp near Preston in April 1915, though a division of the corps remained in England and it is understood that Hinchliffe remained with this contingent. In the February he had been promoted to the rank of captain and was described as popular with the men. However, in June he was arrested and brought before Kirkham Police Court, near Blackpool, charged with stealing a motorcycle and sidecar belonging to a fellow officer. He was also initially charged with two counts of stealing items from a woman at a Blackpool hotel but in both cases the allegations were dropped due to 'lack of evidence of felonious intent'.

From mid-June to early July Captain Hinchliffe was on a leave of absence, refusing to make any statement in connection with the serious charges made against him. He did apply, possibly under pressure, to resign his commission; his commanding officer wrote in Hinchliffe's record: 'In spite of the case being dismissed, very grave suspicion rests on Captain Hinchliffe. It will be obvious that he cannot be allowed to take duty with this unit... There is little doubt that he is an undesirable character.'

The London Gazette in August 1915 reported that he had resigned his commission from the West Lancashire Division on the grounds that his position in the future would be 'most embarrassing'. Whatever the reasons behind his fall from grace with regard to the army, it had little effect on his personal life and on September 10th 1915 Ray Hinchliffe married a young woman called Dorothy Taylor at Broughton St John's Church in Salford, Manchester. The marriage certificate shows he gave his age as twenty-three and Dorothy's age as twenty-one but the marriage was annulled in 1921 on the basis that Dorothy had been under the age of consent (twenty-one) at the time of the ceremony.

Hinchliffe didn't remain a civilian for long. In April 1916 he joined the Royal Naval Air Service as a temporary probationary flight sub-lieutenant training at Redcar, Cranwell and Frieston. He gained his Royal Aero Club flying licence certificate, number 3595, on September 21st of that year.

Those early blots on his military record were more than wiped clean by his skill and bravery as a pilot, although it is argued by some aviation historians that he remained something of a loose cannon. He was soon recognised as an exceptional pilot and employed as an instructor at Cranwell in Lincolnshire, later a Royal Air Force base that played a significant part in his Atlantic attempt with Elsie Mackay. From here he clocked up 1250 flying hours in just over a year.

Hinchliffe was then sent to join 12(N), an operational training unit based at Petite Synthe in France. He spent a week becoming familiar with the Sopwith Camel, a Sopwith triplane and the local environs. An operational posting followed with 10(N) Squadron, which later became 210 Squadron, of the Royal Naval Air Service at Dunkirk during January 1918. In April the Royal Air Force was formed and he was gazetted as a lieutenant, honorary captain and, the following month, formally promoted to the rank.

Whilst with 10(N) he flew as deputy flight leader in W. M. Alexander's C Flight. Alexander later said that in his opinion whilst Hinchliffe was a very skilful pilot, he was also dangerous. In one interview, Alexander said: 'God, he was a good pilot. But he was an oddball. Why, he pinched more stuff around there … we didn't know where the hell everything went.'

It was, perhaps, this perceived recklessness that gave Hinchliffe an edge as a pilot; in the final months of the war he made his name as a Sopwith Camel flying ace and was awarded the Distinguished Flying Cross and the Air Force Cross for his achievements. He took part in daring bombing raids and fierce dog fights with German aircraft, scoring six victories before being almost killed in a crash flying the plane C62 on June 3rd 1918.

A certain mythology has arisen over the years around the accident that cost him the sight in his left eye, including a story that he was injured during a dog fight with the infamous German pilot known as the Red Baron, but there is no evidence for this claim. One very credible theory about the crash comes from research carried out by the Great War specialists the Cross and Cockade Society. They state that Hinch was taking part in a night patrol to intercept German Gotha aircraft in very dark conditions with no moon and light ground mist. Despite these difficulties, he spotted and attacked one plane that had been picked out by the searchlights over Hazebrouck at about 1.45am. The gunners in the well-armed Gotha saw him too and during the attack Hinch was hit by a bullet that shattered the bridge of his nose and blinded him in his left eye. He barely avoided crashing in the dense woodland of the Nieppe Forest, though he did hit trees and crash landed between the forest and Dickebusch Lake.

Yet another less derring-do version has been cited by aviation historian Nick Forder, who has cast doubt on the story that came from Hinchliffe's own log book. He has suggested that W. M. Alexander was posted to Home Establishment on May 29th 1919 and Captain Hinchliffe then took over as leader of C Flight. On June 3rd the squadron operations book states that Lt Baird of C Flight made a forced landing in a cornfield shortly after 7pm. The Camel was repaired on the spot and Hinchliffe elected to fly it back to base. The left tyre came off as he was taking off, the Camel swerved left and turned over. Hinchliffe was seriously injured in the crash and taken to No. 13 Casualty Clearing Station.

This would seem to tally with the version of events quoted by author Ralph Barker in his book *Great Mysteries of the Air*. He wrote that Captain Hinchliffe was asked to recover a Sopwith Camel that had been force-landed by another pilot. During the recovery the plane somersaulted, ending up in a tree. Whatever the circumstances of the crash, one fact remains: Hinchliffe was very badly injured, with some of his injuries possibly the result of his head hitting the twin Vickers machine guns with which the aircraft was armed. He was eventually taken to Lady Hadfield's Red Cross hospital, also known as the Anglo-American, at Wimereux, where his condition was listed as: loss of left eye, compound fracture of the skull, simple fracture of the skull, fracture of both jaws and fracture of left leg and arm. He was initially hospitalised on June 23rd 1918, then invalided home on June 27th, receiving further treatment at a hospital in Hampstead, London. Although he eventually recovered from most of the injuries, he lost the sight of his left eye and for the rest of his life wore a distinctive eye patch.

Whatever mistakes he made as an impetuous young man, Captain Hinchliffe's bravery and determination – whether the result of a dangerous recklessness or not – cannot be questioned. Despite the appalling injuries he suffered, he soon found himself back in the cockpit. Perhaps it took a maverick character to face the dreadful odds that stood before the young men brave enough to take to the air during the First World War.

The loss of his left eye appears to have had little effect initially on the captain's high-flying career. Writing in 1931, aviation expert Charles Dixon described Captain Hinchliffe as: 'probably the only active and certified pilot in the world who had the use of only one eye. He had always to wear a patch over the other, but his disability did not prevent him taking the full responsibility of his position. In fact, his ability proved that he was not partly disabled as a pilot, and he was thereby accepted as having the same standard of fitness as a pilot with normal vision.'

The demands of a hungry war machine meant that remarkable strides had been made in the field of aviation during the First World War, with scientists and designers focussed on creating and improving planes capable of flying and fighting. The end of the war meant that there was a huge surplus of aircraft that had been produced but were no longer needed. These became available, very cheaply, to entrepreneurs who believed in the as-yet-unproven future of the fledgling aviation industry. This set the scene for the rise of air transport and flight as a leisure pastime and as an entertainment, with many 'flying circuses' taking to the air around the country, providing a spectacle of tricks, aerobatics and joy rides. This new, exciting industry had potential and opportunities for budding businessmen who had the skill or the money to take advantage of the situation. Aviators and their backers soon seized on challenges to set new records and establish passenger transport routes. Big money prizes were on offer for those who could fly the highest, the fastest or the furthest.

As one of the most experienced airmen of his generation Captain Hinchliffe, despite his injury, was in a prime position to take advantage of this new field of opportunity. He had experience of flying more than forty different types of aircraft, including Avro, Bleriot, Bristol Fokker, Handley-Page, Sopwith and Vickers. Following demobilisation in 1919, he began his civilian flying career by taking passengers for thrilling joy rides at seaside resorts. There was some controversy when the Air Ministry rejected him as the first pilot of the new London to Paris civil air route on the grounds that a man with only one eye could not judge distance. But this disappointment led to a greater opportunity when he was snapped up by the Avro company, which had started to open centres for pleasure flying – flying clubs – in different parts of Great Britain.

His talent was quickly recognised and, when the little Avro 'Baby' aircraft was sent to Holland, it was Hinch who was asked to accompany the plane to give demonstration flights. In Holland one of the new passenger companies, KLM Royal Dutch Airlines, soon made him an offer and he took up the pilot's seat, which for him was in the co-pilot's position to give him better visibility, in their growing fleet. He made numerous flights for the company, establishing passenger routes all over Europe and testing new aircraft. Such was the respect for his ability and experience as a pilot that his opinion was frequently sought by the company when they were considering new acquisitions. On his recommendations KLM invested in two new Fokker FII aircraft in 1920 at the price of 45,000 guilders and later that year Hinch made the first operational flights to London's Croydon airport.

During his time as chief pilot at KLM Hinch met and married Emilie Gallizien, who was working as the personal secretary to the company's general manager. He called her Milly or M and she called him either Ray or Walter. They went on to have two daughters, Joan and Pamela, the youngest born just a few short months before his attempt to fly the Atlantic.

After KLM Hinch joined Daimler Hire Ltd, taking up a position as Continental Manager first in Paris and later in Amsterdam, running a service between Croydon and Amsterdam and establishing routes between London and Berlin and London and Manchester. When this company was amalgamated with Handley-Page and Instone to form Imperial Airways, the main British civil air service, Hinch naturally joined the new concern and in December 1926 he flew a Hercules aircraft to Cairo to open the company's eastern route.

By association Hinch was also involved with what at the time was the world's worst air disaster and the subsequent enquiry into the crash – the first public enquiry ever held in aviation. The Croydon Air Disaster happened on Christmas Eve 1924 when a plane that Hinch had piloted several times during the previous week on flights to and from Europe failed to lift fully after take-off. It crashed and burst into flames, claiming the lives of all eight passengers and the pilot.

As the usual pilot of the machine, Hinch was called to give evidence at the subsequent enquiry. His reputation as a consummate professional in the field of flight was firmly established. In *The First Croydon Airport 1915–1928*, authors Bob Learmonth, Joanna Nash and Douglas Cluett refer to the fact that the captain's handicap did not impair his passengers' trust in his ability and he was an 'extremely popular pilot'. They quote *The Daily Mail's* air correspondent, Harry Harper, who wrote at the time: 'About Hinchliffe's piloting of an aeroplane there was something – some smooth, masterly power – which definitely put him in a class by himself. Though he was such a superb pilot, Hinchliffe was never satisfied with his own flying. He was always trying to improve his take-offs and landings, always seeking to make some addition to his amazing repertoire of trick flying.'

During his time with Imperial Airways on the London to Paris daily run, he was known as one of the most skilful of all the pilots employed by the company. *The New York Times* said: 'In fog or rain he never failed and could make the exact trip to any point aimed at more quickly and expeditiously than any of his comrades. Hinchliffe was, too, a man who kept himself in the pink of condition. He belonged to a race of Englishmen who are reserved to strangers and resent familiarity and self-advertisement but in character are fine beyond comparison.'

In the post-war period, Ray Hinchliffe certainly proved himself to be one of the best pilots in the British Empire. His expertise was so highly rated that he was frequently asked by journalists for his opinion about other record-breaking flights and the achievements of other aviators, something that must have made him all the more determined to one day to find a place among them. In September 1925 he finally claimed two world records of his own, for the length of time spent in the air and distance flown. Reported by the Australian press, Captain Hinchliffe's arrival at 'the London Air Station' piloting a Napier DH express from Amsterdam meant he had completed 6000 hours of flying during his nine-year career: '…taking an average speed for the numerous different types of airplanes he has flown, he has covered more than half a million miles by air. In flying this distance he has spent the equivalent of 250 entire days, or more than eight months in the air', *The Sydney Sun* claimed.

With such a reputation, it is not surprising that the Honourable Elsie Mackay was not the first person to approach Captain Hinchliffe with an ambition to fly the Atlantic east to west. In 1927 he took a leave of absence from Imperial Airways after being commissioned by the outlandish American businessman Charles Levine to fly him back home from London. An eccentric millionaire and president of the Columbia Aircraft Corporation, Levine had been on board the second plane to fly from America to mainland Europe.

Although he achieved the title of being the first passenger to cross the Atlantic in a heavier-than-air craft, he missed out on the chance to be part of the first ever flight to reach the mainland because of his volatile temperament. Levine argued with Charles Lindbergh, going back on an agreement to allow him to fly one of the Colombia planes on his Atlantic attempt. He then fell into dispute with the original pilot of his own project which led to the plane being grounded due to legal action. During this delay Lindbergh found other sponsors and famously took the honour of being the first person to successfully fly solo across the Atlantic, leaving Levine to be publicly ridiculed by the American press.

By chance, Captain Hinchliffe and his wife were in Paris on the day in May 1927 that Lindbergh landed at Le Bourget to unprecedented scenes of enthusiastic welcome. Lindbergh could barely land because of the crowds. Emilie Hinchliffe later recalled how impressed her husband was by the American's achievement. 'How I envy that man,' she recalled him saying; 'he has done something.'

It wasn't long before Hinch was also given the chance to really make a name for himself. Levine proposed using the same aircraft that had brought him across the Atlantic eastwards, a Bellanca W B 2 called *Miss Columbia*, for the return journey and by doing so becoming the first to fly east to west. However, his hot-headedness and cavalier attitude to protocol caused Clarence Chamberlin, the man who had piloted that first flight, to refuse to attempt the return flight with him on board. Levine quickly had a misunderstanding with his next choice of pilot, a Frenchman called Drouhin, not perhaps that unexpectedly given Levine's temperament and the fact that neither could speak the other's language. This led to Drouhin also withdrawing his services and set in motion another breach of contract dispute. Levine was in hot water yet again, this time with the French aviation authorities.

Like many regular passengers on the flights between London and Paris, Levine soon became familiar with Captain Hinchliffe and his exemplary flying record. In return, the captain was known to be keen to interest rich Americans in the commercial possibilities of creating aviation routes across the USA in the same way that they were being established across Europe and further afield.

Businessman Charles Levine with Captain Hinchliffe.
(photograph courtesty of Laurie Notaro)

Despite Levine's reputation, Captain Hinchliffe leapt at the opportunity to pilot the businessman back to New York. He quickly arranged leave from Imperial and obtained permission for the flight to begin from his old wartime base, RAF Cranwell. However, his working relationship with the American was also fraught with problems. Levine's staff were involved in a series of unpleasant incidents at Cranwell, behaviour that did not sit well with the discipline expected on a military base, and the ground crew were thrown off much to the embarrassment of Captain Hinchliffe.

Feeling the project needed closer supervision, he concluded that, following its gruelling transatlantic flight to Berlin, the Bellanca monoplane was in no fit state to attempt the return journey without further repairs. The fact that it had been flown illegally from France to Croydon by Levine, who was not a qualified pilot, to escape the legal action brought by the French pilot Drouhin, and that it had been landed with great difficulty, had not helped its general state.

Levine had managed to persuade the policeman on guard and a mechanic into helping him push the plane out of the hanger at Le Bourget in order for him to warm up the engine and taxi it around to make sure it was in working order. They watched as the American trundled the plane round the airfield until, at the far end of the runway, he turned the machine into the wind and managed to get it into the air. The speed of the Bellanca, even in the hands of a novice, meant that it soon shook off some of Drouhin's friends who gave chase. News was sent round that Levine might head for Croydon and immediately flights were cancelled, planes pushed back into hangars and passengers kept waiting while the control-tower officials search the skies.

Levine headed for the Channel and found his way towards London and then Croydon, but landing a plane is completely different to getting one in the air. Flying too high and too fast, and discovering he had no runway left with the plane only a few feet off the ground, he changed his mind. Straining the plane and 'every law of aerodynamics', according to one commentator, he managed to climb again. This manoeuvre was repeated several times before a local pilot jumped into a small plane to try and guide Levine down. The Bellanca finally bounced itself to earth in what *The Times* described as 'the most alarming experience which has happened in the memory of the civil aviation traffic officers, regular pilots and the aerodrome staff.'

One of the American's first actions on arrival in England was to announce that he was signing Walter Hinchliffe as his new pilot. Sadly Bertaud Drouhin would suffer the fate of so many airmen: whilst planning his own Atlantic flight the following year in a trimotor Couzinet monoplane, he was killed together with another crewman on a test flight.

With his own relationship with Levine fraught with problems, Hinch suggested making an initial attempt to set a long-distance record by flying to India, a flight that started on September 23rd 1927. His concerns about the condition of the plane were soon borne out and they were forced down by engine trouble in Austria. With the problem repaired, they flew on to see the Schneider Trophy air race at Venice followed by a jaunt to Rome. It was later reported that while they were there Mussolini was so impressed with Captain Hinchliffe's airmanship that he asked to meet him and presented him with a signed photograph of himself.

Levine's wealth and flamboyant lifestyle along with this pugilistic character made him good copy with the reporters of the British press and by association Hinch also found himself featuring in the newspapers on a regular basis at this time. The end of this unlikely partnership was duly reported. The final straw between Hinch, who had lasted longer than most, and his sponsor came when Levine proposed taking his mistress, Mabel Boll, who was known as the Diamond Queen, along on the Atlantic attempt. Miss Boll was one of a number of women, Elsie Mackay included, who during this period were desperate to become the first woman to cross the Atlantic in an aeroplane. As colourful a character as her lover, with a glamorous and somewhat scandalous reputation, she could not fly herself and was dependent on finding someone to be the pilot for her ambitions. Learning of Levine's plans to return to New York by plane, Miss Boll ingratiated herself into the project. Captain Hinchliffe was not willing to go along with this change in plan. He point blank refused to allow her to join the flight, saying he was against women participating in aviation. By taking this stand, he found himself out of a job.

Hinch's return to Imperial was not warmly welcomed by his bosses, who had opposed him taking leave of absence and had only agreed after he had threatened to resign altogether. They showed their displeasure through the allocation of work. Pilots then were paid by the hours they spent in the air and Hinch found himself standing around waiting while the most remunerative runs were allocated to less-experienced pilots. For a pilot of his standing, this was not only humiliating but also a disaster financially. He was desperately in need of money as he had used some of his personal funds for expenses when he was working for Levine and, with the prospect of successfully flying the Atlantic, he had commissioned the building of a home for his family in Purley in Surrey.

Ray Hinchliffe with his wife Emilie.
(photograph courtesty of Laurie Notaro)

Despite these disappointments *The New York Times* reported that he never complained even though: 'not only his hopes but his livelihood went down in disaster when Levine's plane crashed near Vienna'. All Hinchliffe thought about was trying again with a different backer to realise what was, to him, an adventure which would be to the 'honour of all airmen and of England.'

For Captain Hinchliffe the options were running out; there were rumours of rule changes at Imperial Airways which might mean there was no long-term future for him with the company. It was at this point, according to the same newspaper, that Hinch realised he had one course of action: to interest someone in financing a transatlantic attempt. The fame and financial reward from such a flight would enable him to interest American backers in starting a passenger airline in that country. It was just at this time that a representative of the Honourable Elsie Mackay approached Captain W. G. R. Hinchliffe with a proposal to finance just such a flight.

CHAPTER FOUR

A 'demonstration of human courage and skill battling against the dangers of a still unknown element'

The extraordinary post-war period of the 1920s and 30s has been given a number of names, the Jazz Age, Age of Swing and Age of the Flapper among them. Although it would prove to be a time of economic depression and great difficulty for many people suffering from the aftermath of the war, it was also an era of feverish, youthful vitality and change. Young people shrugged off the stiffness of the Edwardian period as hemlines climbed to previously unthinkable levels, and many threw caution aside to dance the *Charleston* and the *Black Bottom*. The glamour of film caught the imagination of every class of society.

The position of women changed radically during the First World War. In 1928, as a result of many years of campaigning, women over the age of twenty-one were finally granted the vote on the same terms as men. Further advances for women were being seen in business, law, architecture, sport, motoring and aviation.

Media interest in aviation was at its height in the 1920s and the excitement generated by record breakers and pioneers in this field spread throughout the world. The race was on for pilots to be the fastest, to fly the highest or furthest, or establish longer endurance records. Flight was new, exciting and frequently dangerous, which all added up to a very newsworthy subject. Pioneering pilots were treated as heroes and the general public followed their careers closely. Those who were successful were showered with fame and fortune.

According to historians Glen Jeansomme and David Luhrssen, the '...

fervour greeting Charles A. Lindbergh on his arrival in Paris on May 21st 1927 was not unlike the first landing on the moon four decades later. Lindbergh symbolised the triumph of technology over geography and the human spirit over the barrier of space.' Captain Lindbergh was taken on a tour of European capital cities and was given a tickertape reception on his return to New York.

Despite arriving after Lindbergh, Chamberlain and Levine were also greeted with extraordinary enthusiasm in Germany where their flight eventually officially landed, setting a new distance record and making the millionaire scrap dealer the first passenger to fly the Atlantic. The following year, Amelia Earhart found herself dubbed 'Lady Lindy' after her crossing as a passenger; she received contracts for a book, magazine articles and lecture tours along with endorsements for sportswear, luggage and stationery. She even had a car engine named after her.

Both Captain Hinchliffe and the Honourable Elsie Mackay were already familiar with this level of interest from newspaper and radio reporters, Hinch through his fame as a pilot and association with Levine and Elsie through her society profile and careers in acting and with P&O. Press attention was the last thing Elsie wanted, though, as she was desperate to keep her dreams of flying the Atlantic a secret from her father who, she was confident, would do everything in his considerable power to stop her. Lord Inchcape's fears for his daughter's safety were, of course, not without justification. Accidents happened frequently in aviation without racking up the odds even further by attempting incredibly dangerous flights.

The fly boys of the early commercial routes often continued with that devil-may-care attitude they had established as pilots during the First World War. The risks and dangers seemed to be part of their life blood and, despite the fact that they were now involved in transporting wealthy members of the public, many seemed unable to shed their reckless and competitive natures. Frederick Frank Reilly Minchin, who would be lost in another Atlantic attempt involving a woman, was an RAF veteran and friend of Captain Hinchliffe. A friendly, though ultimately dangerous, rivalry existed between many of these early commercial pilots as they tried to outdo each other when the flights became somewhat routine – 'bus driving', as some called it.

Despite the arduous and often dangerous conditions involved even in cross-Channel flights, pilots began to vie with one another to record the fastest times. In August 1924 Hinch recorded in his log book that he had managed to overtake Minchin's plane by taking a short cut; six months later he wrote of another race: 'Managed to beat Minchin in DH50 by 7 minutes.'

A competition between the two men to beat the London to Paris record in June 1927 ended in near disaster for Minchin – and his passengers. He was piloting a W9a Hampstead with nine passengers on board on a routine flight from Paris to Croydon when he ran out of fuel and attempted a crash landing in a field, narrowly missing a house but striking a small copse of trees, which damaged the starboard wings and undercarriage. The crew and passengers all escaped severely rattled but luckily without injury. When an Air Ministry accident investigation discovered that the pilot had run out of fuel because he had flown considerably faster than normal cruising speed, had failed to make use of the plane's fuel economiser and had not kept a watch on the fuel tanks, he was dismissed. It was clear that Captain Minchin had been attempting to catch an Argosy plane that had taken off on the same route twenty-five minutes earlier – a plane piloted by his old friend and rival Captain Hinchliffe.

Oddly, this accident played a significant part in the destinies of the two men. At the time of the crash, Captain Minchin was involved in a plan with another Imperial Airways colleague, Robert McIntosh, to buy a new Fokker aircraft at a cost of £3000 with the intention of being the first to fly the Atlantic east to west (from London to New York) and then, after an eight-hour break, fly back again. *The Daily Express* believed that the flight would start from RAF Cranwell, where the runway was being specially lengthened. They had raised half of the necessary funds from two wealthy backers, American William B. Leeds and the Honourable Elsie Mackay, but their failure to find the rest of the cash, and possibly Minchin's irresponsible episode resulting in the crash, meant that the plan never got off the ground.

The lure of the Atlantic was, in the majority of cases, the promise of personal fame and financial reward, for the commercial world had become extravagantly generous towards its flying heroes. According to aviation author C. St John Sprigg, these incentives were only part of the story. Writing in 1935 in his book *Great Flights*, he said: 'It is impossible to imagine any more difficult, dangerous, uncertain, or worrying way of making money than by long distance flying: and any man who has flown the Atlantic must have in him a part of the spirit that inspires the mountaineer and the Polar explorer, whatever other motives may be mixed with it. The justification of long-distance flying is its demonstration of human courage and skill battling against the dangers of a still unknown element.' The North Atlantic seemed to present the most obvious challenge to the growing aviation community in Europe and North America. Separating two continents from coast to coast, the sea stretches for 1900 miles, unbroken by any refuge for the pilot. The Atlantic Ocean also produces the world's worst flying weather for at its centre the warm Gulf Stream mixes with the icy North Equatorial Current, creating rainstorms, sudden gales and a huge drifting mass of fog.

It would take a particular kind of courage and determination to even attempt to cross such an expanse. Even today pilots remain respectful of the Atlantic. At air-company operation centres computer screens, charts and maps forecasting the weather remain in the background of every flight. In his book Atlantic, author Simon Winchester said: 'The great ocean is still held very much in awe. Great seas are not kindly entities over which to fly: if your aircraft somehow fails, where, exactly, do you put down? No pilot leaves the chocks for a transoceanic flight without remembering the first axiom in flight school: take off is voluntary, but landing is compulsory. And in the middle of the ocean it is self-evidently true not just that there is nowhere to land, but that there just is no land. No land at all. Those who pioneered the practice of flying over sea water knew that all too well.' According to Simon Winchester the Atlantic is described by the two air-traffic control centres in charge of the airspace as a region 'moderately hostile to civilian air traffic' due to its vastness and the fact that there are no navigational aids and no communication relays.

Even now, a century after those early flights, the situation remains that: 'for a substantial portion of the journey over the ocean a civilian transport aircraft is essentially on its own. It gets into trouble out in mid-sea, then it is in big trouble indeed.' Simon Winchester said: 'What might appear to a safely arrived passenger as no more than quotidian routine is in fact the result of planning sessions no less intense than for a truly white-knuckled adventure, like rounding Cape Horn or scaling Mount Everest's South Col.'

In 1928 to attempt this journey was spectacularly daring under the most favourable conditions, even more so due to the fragility and limited range of the aircraft available at that time. Mr Sprigg argued that the long-distance flier was a rare bird: 'He must have the judgement and nerve to be able to get a heavily loaded machine off the ground and land accurately when tired and jaded. The great flights have been made by men of pronounced organising ability, who went into all details of the flight, and sought out the latest aircraft and equipment but without the foolish delusion that by taking enough precautions a dangerous flight could be made safe. That is not the spirit of the record breaker.'

By 1927 it seemed as if everyone involved in aviation had been overcome by Atlantic fever; the race was on to cross the ocean from America or Canada to Europe. Celebrated pilot Jim Mollison noted in his *Book of Famous Flyers* that many in North America seemed to have completely forgotten that Alcock and Brown had already achieved the title 'first' and believed the honour was still up for grabs. But '...tragedy followed fast in the wake of these plucky if somewhat rash contestants,' he wrote, '...by September of that year twenty-one lives had been lost, aeroplanes and passengers disappearing amidst the wastes of the ocean.'

Some didn't make it any further than the runway. With these small planes packed to the gunnels with fuel and weighed down by this load, it would prove to be a fearsome challenge just to get into the air, even for the most experienced pilot. In 1926 an attempt by French war ace Renee Fonck crashed on take-off at Roosevelt Field in New York. Miraculously he escaped, along with one crewman, but two others were caught in the flames as the plane turned into a giant fireball.

In May 1927 Captain Lindbergh set the standard by flying solo from

New York to Paris in the single-engine monoplane *Spirit of St Louis*. He was closely followed by Clarence Chamberlain, carrying Charles Levine as the first passenger to fly the Atlantic from New York to Germany, beating Lindbergh's recently established distance record.

Many attempts were highly reliant on luck and that was certainly the case with the Chamberlain/Levine flight. Not long after take-off from New York on 4th June the crew discovered that their earth induction compass was wrong; suddenly having to rely on a magnetic compass meant that for the rest of the flight they only had a hazy idea of where they were. They were feeling anxious before they even crossed the eastern seaboard but, reluctant to face the ridicule of the aviation community, they decided to keep going. In the afternoon they spotted and identified a ship as the *Mauretania* and, thanks to a copy of *The New York Times* that they happened to have on board which included the shipping news, they were able to work out the liner's approximate speed and make a guess that they were, by then, somewhere near Ireland. Soon afterwards they spotted land but also hit bad weather, which forced them to climb. They were seen flying over Cornwall and Plymouth and also places in Normandy, Holland and Saxony. They eventually ran out of fuel 100 miles from Berlin, having been in the air for forty-one hours and having flown 3905 miles.

Chamberlain's achievement made quite an impact on popular culture and they had a rapturous reception in Berlin. The novelist Dorothy L. Sayers referred to the flight in her 1927 book *Unnatural Death*, knowing her readers would be well aware of it. The thrill of this new technology was used again by the author in her novel *Clouds of Witness*, when her famous sleuth Lord Peter Wimsey is dramatically flown from Paris to Croydon (a regular Hinchliffe run) in order to appear in the nick of time at his brother's trial. Although two further flights were successfully completed in 1927, from New York to Normandy and Newfoundland to Croydon, there were many attempts that were accused of being hasty, ill-advised and having no justification in aeronautical terms. In the opinion of Charles Dixon, who wrote *The Conquest of the Atlantic by Air* in 1931, many people responsible had no legitimate link with aviation: '...professional airmen engaged by them were led to a premature death through the inadequacy of their preparations. Women in particular were fascinated by the glory and consequently responsible for more than one attempt, all except two leading to tragedy for themselves and their crews.'

The comparatively easier west–east route claimed its victims and was more difficult than the successful (or lucky) flights suggested. An attempt in 1919 by Harry Hawker and Commander Mackenzie Grieve in a Sopwith biplane to fly from New York to England ended with a forced landing in the middle of the Atlantic; the intrepid pair had the good fortune to be rescued.

There were many unsuccessful attempts from the first in 1910 with Walter Wellman and crew on board an airship, but the majority were over a ten-year period between 1924 and 1934, with the largest cluster during 1927 and 1928. A number of these flights involved women; one or two were perhaps foolish and that was enough for the male-dominated world to tar all subsequent flights by women with the same brush. Charles Dixon's comment implies that women were the cause of some of these tragic failures, throwing away the lives of the experienced male pilots, yet the majority of flights crewed only by men that also failed tragically did not come in for the same criticism.

Levine and Chamberlain's flight was ill equipped and extremely foolish; it was driven forward by fear of ridicule and only successful because of an excellent plane design plane. They had more than their fair share of luck – and extraordinary stamina on the pilot's part – yet they were heralded as heroes. Even some modern women aviation writers have sadly fallen into the same well-worn misogyny; early authors dismissed the flights of Princess Lowenstein and Elsie Mackay, in particular, as the foolish whims of rich women looking for novelty. In her book *Women of the Air* Judy Lomax dismisses both women in just a paragraph saying that they 'had more money than luck, or perhaps sense'.

It was perhaps the publicity and the pre-flight antics of American Ruth Elder that distracted the public from her real skills as a pilot and set the tone for the dismissive attitude towards women flyers. Miss Elder had been training as a pilot for some time before her Atlantic attempt in October 1927 with her instructor Captain George Haldeman. Without a private income to support such a flight, Miss Elder had to attract sponsorship. As she was an attractive young woman, this involved a lot of glamorous photographs of her posing with her plane, named *The American Girl*, which were used widely in the US press. She was quoted as saying that she intended landing in Paris 'dressed to kill' and took a box of beauty preparations and diamond rings with her on the flight; certainly she always had her lipstick to hand. Experienced airman George Haldeman took an equal role in the flight but, when it failed, it was Miss Elder who received the full force of the subsequent criticism. Charles Dixon, who was working as an aviation journalist at the time, said: 'In view of the risks the pair deliberately faced they may have the honour of being the luckiest of all who wrestled the ocean.'

The pair ignored advice to wait for more favourable weather but they were beset by delays for days on end and they were fully aware of the plans of rival Frances Grayson, who was also determined to be the first woman to cross the Atlantic aiming for Copenhagen, though in her case as a passenger. When they took off from New York, a storm had been forecast and they made little real effort to navigate accurately so that when an oil pipe broke in their Stinson Detroiter they were so far off course that they were almost as far south as the Azores. Forced down into the sea, they were incredibly lucky to be rescued by a Dutch tanker.

Miss Elder's reputation as a serious pilot took a further knock when the ship's captain reported that, despite having been in considerable danger and having just been plucked in swelling seas from a sinking plane, the bedraggled young woman made finding a mirror and lipstick her first priority.

Taken to the Azores, Miss Elder came into contact, quite by chance, with another woman aviator who had also been set on crossing the Atlantic, this time from east to west but by the southern route in stages. The Austrian actress Frau Lilli Dillenz and her crew of three German airmen only got as far as Horta before the attempt was abandoned due to terrible weather conditions.

Ruth Elder and Captain Haldeman eventually arrived in Paris but by more traditional transport. On their return to the United States, Miss Elder was rewarded with a highly lucrative vaudeville tour and later a movie contract, leading to allegations that this had always been her aim and their flight was simply an elaborate and foolish publicity stunt. 'They had wandered over the Atlantic for 36 hours and covered over 3000 miles which would have landed them well into Europe if they had known how to navigate!' commented Charles Dixon at the time. Ruth Elder continued with her love of flying and took part in the first National Women's Air Derby in 1929, finishing a very creditable fourth.

Ruth Elder.
(photograph courtesy of Lauri Notaro)

Ruth Elder's rival, successful businesswoman Mrs Frances Grayson, met the same grim fate that greeted so many Atlantic aviators. Her aim was to fly from Maine to Europe in a twin-engine Sikorsky amphibian aircraft, built for the attempt, called *The Dawn*. Copenhagen was the target, due to their sponsor Mrs Aage Ancker being of Danish extraction.

The first two attempts, driven by Grayson's fear that Ruth Elder would beat her to the title of first woman to fly the Atlantic, soon ran into problems when the plane, weighed down by fuel, failed to lift off. A third effort saw them travel further but the plane began to lose height due to problems with the port engine. The pilot, Wilmer Stulz, known as Bill, had to offload fuel to prevent the machine and crew from descending into the waves. During this flight there was a dramatic dispute between the highly experienced Stulz and the navigator, Brice Goldsborough, who, along with Mrs Grayson – whose knowledge of flying was pretty rudimentary – wished to continue with the flight. Stulz refused to go on and turned the plane back towards safety, returning them to Maine. On landing he immediately resigned and refused to contemplate flying with Frances Grayson again. She, however, was not deterred by the loss of her pilot. Having hired Norwegian Lieutenant Oskar Omdal to join the navigator and mechanic Fred Schroeder, they took off again from Roosevelt Field on Christmas Eve 1927 into what was known to be quite appalling weather, with the aim of landing in Newfoundland in order to set off across the Atlantic from there the following day.

It was reported that the determined Mrs Grayson had taken a small revolver in her handbag, presumably to deal with any mutinous behaviour from her crew on this flight. Perhaps it was her zeal to become the 'first' that blinded her to the lunacy of making the flight at that time of year. Despite extensive air searches over the following weeks, the plane and crew were never seen again – although late the following year an engine was recovered from the ocean bed by a fishing boat about forty miles south of Cape Cod that was believed to be part of the missing plane.

The following year Bill Stulz piloted the plane *The Friendship* across the Atlantic with passenger Amelia Earhart on board, enabling her to claim the title cherished by so many – that of being the first woman to cross the Atlantic by a heavier-than-air craft.

The first attempt on the Atlantic by a woman was actually made by a British princess in the August of 1927 and preceded the flights of Elder and Grayson. Princess Anne Loewenstein-Wertheim commissioned Hinchliffe's old daredevil flying chum, Lieutenant-Colonel Frederick Minchin, to join her regular pilot Flying Officer Leslie Hamilton to fly the Fokker monoplane the *St Raphael*. The flight came during a period when numerous failed Atlantic attempts by male pilots, and subsequent loss of life, was causing widespread concern and consternation.

Following Lindbergh's success there was an almost feverish amount of aerial activity, fuelled by the fascination of the public and the press – the first ones also to condemn the flights for their loss of life. 'Hardly a day passed but the world's newspapers chronicled the departure, the progress, the spectacular landing or the equally spectacular failure of a long-distance flyer,' stated authors Clifford Collinson and Captain E. McDermott in their 1934 book *Through Atlantic Clouds*.

The loss of life began to cause a groundswell of opinion against the Atlantic flights, with many people concerned not only at the deaths of the flyers but also at the cost to the public purse of the resulting searches. The aeronautical journal *Airways* consulted some of the leading figures in aviation at the time and discovered a sharp divergence of opinion. Some, including Aviation Minister Sir Sefton Brancker, believed that decisions should be left to the pilots involved whilst others, such as the designer and manufacturer A. V. Roe, were opposed to further attempts until better machines and understanding of the weather conditions could be achieved.

The flight of the *St Raphael* added fuel to those concerned about this widespread Atlantic fever. Despite a blessing by the Archbishop of Cardiff before take-off from Upavon aerodrome at 7.15am on August 31st, the plane and its occupants, like so many others, went missing without trace. Hopes had been high for the success of this flight, given the great experience of the pilot; in addition, an oil tanker sighted the plane at 9.44pm that night at least half way across, with a further report from a Dutch tanker the following morning that 'something' was seen flying 420 miles from New York.

The known target on this occasion was the Canadian city of Ottawa and, at this news, preparations began to welcome the first woman to fly the Atlantic. But the plane, like so many others, was never seen again. Despite many saying that there was no pilot more likely to succeed than Minchin, it was the sixty-year-old female passenger who came in for the blanket criticism that flights involving women were ill-advised and foolish.

The following month another Fokker monoplane was sponsored by American newspaper magnate Randolph Hearst from Maine with Rome as its destination. The crew of three, including one of Hearst's editors, was on a mission to deliver a wreath in memory of two French airmen who had lost their lives earlier in the year trying to fly from east to west. Sadly, the Hearst crew suffered the same fate as the crew they were attempting to commemorate; wreckage of their plane was later found off the Newfoundland coast. On the same day two Canadians flying from Newfoundland were similarly lost, but this time with no further trace.

With the loss of the Grayson flight in December 1927, the toll of deaths on Atlantic flights following the success of Captain Lindbergh in May rose to twelve, not including three others lost on a South Atlantic route and four killed by accidents on take-off.

Along with the concern and criticism of these Atlantic adventures, there was also extensive discussion in the aviation community about why so many flights were failing and ending in disaster. Looking back from a modern perspective, it seems somewhat miraculous that any of these small, fragile planes made it at all. Of course during this period the technology involved in aircraft construction was cutting edge and there was every expectation – at least on the part of the pilots – that the flights would succeed. The speculation and theorising pointed in part to the notorious fog banks off Newfoundland, which were believed to be a major contributory factor in the failures, along with the high, persistent headwinds for those attempting to fly west.

Although weather conditions could be gauged near the coastlines of North

America and Europe, what was happening in the middle of the Atlantic could only be guessed at even by the most experienced meteorologists. Edward Jablonski, author of *Atlantic Fever*, wrote that whilst a safe transatlantic flight took 'much preparation, nearly superhuman skill, a worthy aircraft and an incalculable quantity of pure luck' not every engine was reliable or aircraft fit for purpose, whilst 'few pilots, motivated by a taste for adventure and emboldened by courage, had the inclination to learn navigation. And all too many were all but ignorant of the winds, clouds and weathers over the Atlantic until it was too late.'

Aviation author Charles Dixon felt that, considering all the conditions, the westward route was a 'far more hazardous adventure than the easterly flight and airmen did not face it so readily.' In the opinion of C. St John Spriggs, one of the worst dangers for long-distance aviators was simply losing their way. 'Over the desert, or at night, or out at sea or when flying above cloud and fog, the pilot is at the mercy of the wind. An error of a few miles either way may cause an aircraft to miss its aerodrome and go on flying indefinitely until petrol fails. This, no doubt, has been the cause of many transatlantic "mysteries".'

Fatigue was also a major factor in the struggle to conquer the Atlantic westwards. 'Continuous bad weather, with its bumps and its anxiety, and its periods of blind flying takes a tremendous toll of the flier,' wrote Mr Spriggs. He argued in his book *Great Flights* that blind flying presented a particular challenge to the Atlantic aviator: 'When an aircraft is flying in fog and cloud the pilot has no horizon to guide him and so can no longer make the continual sight correcting movements which are necessary in flight, just as they are in riding a bicycle. Without these corrections the aeroplane will, sooner or later, get into a spin, from which the pilot has no notion how to extricate it. It is, in fact, like trying to ride a bicycle blindfold along a narrow plank.'

It was against this backdrop of controversy, opposition, losses, lucky escapes and tragedies that Elsie Mackay approached Captain Hinchliffe with a view to making their own daring attempt to fly across the treacherous Atlantic Ocean.

CHAPTER FIVE

The Most Secret Flight
in the History of Aviation

It was in the genteel surroundings of a luncheon party at the sumptuous Ritz Hotel in London in October 1927 that the Honourable Elsie Mackay first spoke to Captain Hinchliffe about her burning desire to be the first woman to fly the Atlantic.

Elsie had originally consulted her friend Anthony Joynson-Wreford about the best way to find a suitable pilot for the proposed flight. Joynson-Wreford had suffered his own dose of Atlantic fever; earlier in the year he'd made extensive preparations for an attempt, along with Scottish flyer Captain Robert McIntosh, another friend of Captain Hinchliffe's at Imperial Airways. His involvement in the flight ended when Captain McIntosh decided that he needed someone able to take turns as pilot, something Joynson-Wreford was unable to do for lengthy periods because of a war wound to the knee.

McIntosh went on to make a westward attempt with the Irish airman Commander James Fitzmaurice, a man whose future plans would have a fatal role to play in the Hinchliffe and Mackay story. This flight, in September 1927, set off from Baldonnel Airport near Dublin in a single-engine Fokker named Princess Xenia after the wife of their sponsor, the American businessman William R. Leeds, who had been a financial supporter, along with Elsie Mackay, of McIntosh's project with Fred Minchin mentioned in the previous chapter. The Scots/Irish attempt didn't get far; flying into atrocious weather conditions they were defeated by headwinds and, in an appalling storm, they finally managed to land on a beach near Ballybunion.

It was Joynson-Wreford who came up with the name of Captain Hinchliffe and it was he who introduced Elsie to the tall, dashing, one-eyed pilot at The Ritz, a meeting also attended by Elsie's bank manager. Elsie put her cards on the table, a trait for straight talking that she had inherited from her father. She needed complete discretion; everyone was sworn to secrecy. Although she knew that the captain was against women being involved with aviation – he had turned down the offer of £10,000 to take Mabel Boll on the flight with Levine – Elsie was a rich, beautiful, accomplished screen actress; she could be very persuasive and was used to getting her own way.

The deal presented to Hinch proved hard to resist, despite his reservations. Elsie offered to finance a trip to the US to purchase a plane of his own choice plus a generous wage of £80 a month and all expenses paid. She guaranteed to give him all the prize money they would win and, on top of all that, she would insure his life for £10,000 as a security if anything went wrong. This was a small fortune, far more than he could ever earn at Imperial Airways even if the sight in his remaining eye stayed good for some years. By comparison, a train driver in 1928 earned about £3 10s a week and a woman mill-worker took home just over £1 a week.

In return for this generous wage, Elsie required absolute secrecy along with his agreement that she would not only accompany him on the flight but she would also be co-pilot. Hinchliffe returned from the glamorous surroundings of The Ritz in bustling central London to the quiet Surrey village where he lived with Emilie, who was by then expecting their second child, to discuss the offer. He was only too aware that he had a family to support and he had to find the money to complete the house that was being built for them. The income from Imperial Airways was always going to be limited and he knew that his career as a pilot was entirely dependent on the sight of one eye. Not only that, the airline's standards and rules were changing, leaving a further question mark over his future with the company. His bosses had been unimpressed by him taking leave for the Levine fiasco and he knew that they would not sanction another leave of absence.

Emilie Hinchliffe later revealed that her husband secretly suffered a dread of losing the sight in his remaining eye that would make it impossible for him to provide for his family as a pilot. This had been the subject of many private discussions between them. Taking Miss Mackay's offer would mean putting all his eggs in one basket. He knew the risks; he'd lost friends and colleagues during the previous year to this dangerous adventure but risk taking had become part of the life blood of these young men who had flown during World War One.

Hinch was an experienced and confident pilot and a successful Atlantic flight, something he had absolute faith he could achieve, would mean fortune, glory and a stable future for his family. He would be able to pocket the prize money that was still on offer for such an achievement and, through his proven credentials, interest rich Americans in investing in the development of civil aviation within the US. The flight with Miss Mackay could enable him to make enough money to retire from active flying and he would no longer have to fear the loss of his sight. His confidence in his experience and ability as a pilot made him feel that this was an opportunity he couldn't turn down, and his wife's faith in his flying was equal to his own.

After agreeing to Elsie's terms, Hinch proved to be an excellent accomplice in the secret plan. Elsie did everything she could to prevent her family – and in particular her father – from discovering her ambition. She knew that if she were discovered Lord Inchcape would not only forbid her to fly but he could also impound her bank account and bring his considerable influence to bear on any airman associated with the project.

Elsie adopted a scheme whereby the money needed was not drawn on her own account but in the name of a friend. Although Hinch had a reputation for keeping his cards close to his chest, he had gained a level of fame through his own achievements in the air. His association with Charles Levine had attracted a good deal of interest in the American press so when he arrived in New York in December 1927, the city's newspaper reporters kept a keen eye on his movements.

A number of rumours preceded his arrival but, luckily, all of them were wide of the mark. Some believed that he had travelled to New York to sort out money owed to him by Levine whilst another story figured that he was being hired by the notorious businessman's mistress Diamond Queen Mabel Boll to pilot her ambition of being the first woman to cross the Atlantic by air. The glamorous blonde heiress had set her heart on this title and, ever since her return from Europe following Hinchliffe's refusal to pilot the *Miss Colombia* with her on board, she had been trying to buy the services of someone to fly her across the ocean for $25,000. Aviation journalists, and Miss Boll herself, presumed that the captain had changed his mind and was travelling to America to take up the offer. But, when asked about his voyage by *The New York Times*, Captain Hinchliffe smoothly asserted that he was there simply for his health: 'solely to benefit an attack of quinsy [a severe infection of the throat and tonsils].' He told reporters that when he became subject to an attack of the illness, he had managed to obtain a few days leave from his position with Imperial Airways in order to make the convalescent sea trip. He insisted that this was the only reason for his journey and that he expected to return immediately on board the *Berengaria* because, during the voyage, he had learned that his wife had given birth to their second daughter back in England and he needed to hurry home to spend Christmas with his family.

What the reporters didn't know was that Hinch had travelled to the US on the White Star liner, *Cedric*. With the help of his friend John Cummings, who was a purser on the ship, he had been able to disembark at Boston in secret and complete his business before the reporters learned that he had arrived in America. Mr Cummings later told *The New York Times* that he had been one of a small circle of personal friends who had known the real reason for the trip and the plan to fly the Atlantic with Miss Mackay.

Captain Hinchliffe met with Bill Mara, the secretary-treasurer of the Stinson Aircraft Corporation, to negotiate the purchase of one of their high-wing Detroiter monoplanes. According to John W. Underwood, author of *The Stinsons*, when Hinch told Mara of his intention to make the east–west journey the businessman told him angrily to 'cut your own throat right now and you'll save yourself and everyone else a lot of trouble.'

Following this initial rebuff Elsie and Hinch agreed to change their story, insisting that they had reconsidered and would make a record attempt on a distance flight to India instead, a story that would be repeated to the press over the coming months.

At a second meeting with Bill Mara, the captain was able to finally make the purchase, but only by agreeing to the condition that the machine would be flown on a record attempt over land. The Stinson Detroiter was only thirty-two feet long with disc wheels, a tail skid and a single Wright Whirlwind 220 horsepower J-5C radial engine, the type that had already proven its reliability on a number of long-distance flights, including those of Lindbergh and Chamberlain. The machine itself had been the plane of choice for a number of flyers over the previous year because of its track record. At sea level, and with a regular number of passengers, crew and fuel load, it could reach speeds of 122 miles per hour. It stood just over eight feet high with a large and robust wingspan of forty-five feet ten inches and an area of 219 square feet. The enclosed cockpit gave dual controls and the cabin was roomy and would ordinarily seat six passengers, although *The Manchester Guardian's* aviation correspondent told readers that the plane carried a pilot, three passengers and 300lbs of baggage. The fuselage was of a steel tubular construction, giving a long and roomy profile, and it also featured a thick section designed for speed with high lifting power.

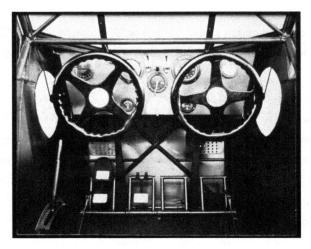

The cockpit of a Stinson Detroiter like the *Endeavour*.
(photograph courtesy The Golden Wings Flying Museum, Minneapolis USA)

The Detroiter had originally been an innovatively designed biplane but pioneer designer and aircraft manufacturer Eddie Stinson had realised in 1926 that biplanes were obsolete. The design was overhauled and reborn as a monoplane but, unusually, the plane retained the name of the earlier machine.

In 1927 the SM-1 Detroiter had easily beaten all comers in the two week Ford Tour race, establishing the plane as the leader in its field. John W. Underwood wrote: 'It has been said the Detroiter monoplanes were kept very busy making history and that just about every one built was off on some sort of record flight. The SM-1 Detroiter was clearly a very capable machine that would bring its crew home given a little luck and tolerable weather.'

The plane bought by Captain Hinchliffe for Elsie Mackay was shipped back to the United Kingdom aboard the *Aquitania* and assembled at the famous Brooklands aerodrome by the engineers at Messrs Vickers, where it was also fitted out for a long-distance flight. Brooklands motor racing track and airfield at Weybridge in Surrey was an ideal base for Captain Hinchliffe, who had his family home in the county; it was also a place that held strong ties for him as he had taken his first flying lessons there before the war. This was where Tommy Sopwith had developed and first flown his Pup and Camel biplanes. It was Captain Hinchliffe's talent as a flier of the Sopwith Camel that had brought him such success during the war, ending his service as an 'ace'. It was in one of the wooden sheds, known as Brooklands Flying Village, that the Stinson Detroiter, now named the *Endeavour* by Miss Mackay, began to take shape.

Captain Hinchliffe shared the conviction with his wife and Miss Mackay that it was not only feasible but relatively straightforward to fly the Atlantic, as long as sufficient careful preparations were made. As a responsible and devoted father of a young family, he had no intention of taking any unnecessary risks with his own life or that of Miss Mackay. He had already made exhaustive plans for his flight with Charles Levine, including extensive calculations, and he now continued and recalculated these for the new attempt.

In January 1928 he left the employ of Imperial Airways and was officially engaged by Elsie Mackay as her personal pilot. He not only devoted all of his time to the preparation of the plane but he also began instructing his new employer on various aspects of flying that she would not have come across before but that she would need on an Atlantic crossing, including the skills to use a long-distance compass.

Work began in earnest, adapting the Stinson Detroiter for the gruelling journey ahead. The plane's passenger seats were removed and a large tank, which would hold 225 gallons of fuel, was installed in the resulting space behind the cockpit. Hinch had worked out that with a crew of two the *Endeavour* could lift a total of 480 gallons, giving a flying time of fifty hours and a range of 5000 miles – easily enough to get them to North America. The wing tanks carried a standard load of 180 gallons and the remaining fuel was stacked in seventeen specially commissioned aluminium cans, each holding four and a half gallons. The canisters were manufactured to be much lighter – two and a half pounds lighter – than normal fuel containers and they weighed less than a pound when empty. The canisters had also been designed so that the stopper of one fitted into the socket of another, making storage easier and, of vital importance, more stable.

When it came to positioning these tanks, room had to be left to allow access so that Hinch could clamber back in order to fill the cabin tank using the cans during the flight. The plan was to simply throw the empty cans out of the door. There was quite a bit of trial and error before a suitable method of stacking was decided on. Another difficulty was that the carburettor was gravity fed from the wing tanks so that all the petrol stored in the cabin had to be pumped into the wing tanks first. This involved a mechanical pump, driven by an engine, and two hand devices, which were fitted into the plane, leaving an elaborate labyrinth of arterial piping in the cabin behind Captain Hinchliffe's seat on the right of the cockpit. The wing tanks, when empty, could serve as buoyancy helping to keep the plane afloat if they were forced to descend into the sea. Including the weight of the empty cans, the total load of the fuel would weigh 3456lbs. Fully laden, the cruising speed would be reduced from 122 miles per hour to ninety.

Some aviation writers believed that Joynson-Wreford had an interest in the venture beyond simply doing the introductions and that he thought he would be part of the flight until almost the last minute. It seems, given the extensive planning and details of the need to use every inch of the plane for fuel storage other than the dual controls in the cockpit and Hinchliffe's calculations based on a crew of two, this was never really on the cards. Perhaps Joynson-Wreford secretly hoped that Elsie Mackay would drop out of the flight either due to family pressure or fear of what lay ahead and he could then take her place in the cockpit.

Captain Hinchliffe's absolute commitment to the flight's success cannot be doubted. In her book *The Return of Captain W. G. R. Hinchliffe* Emilie recalled: 'My husband knew full well the risk inseparable from such a flight. Preparations – extending over a period of nearly twelve months – were complete and absolutely exhaustive as to detail. Past weather reports of the general conditions prevailing over the Atlantic at the time of year contemplated for the commencement of the flight, were studied. Charts were procured, alternative courses plotted on them in collaboration with Air Ministry experts.'

Regarding the plane itself, Mrs Hinchliffe wrote of how her husband supervised every aspect of the assembly of the machine. 'Right up to the time of the machine's completion and readiness for test, my husband was constantly at the aerodrome.' His dedication continued with test flights: 'Her cruising and top speed were ascertained, the efficacy of the petrol system and the emergency provisions relative thereto were tested repeatedly and in addition, petrol consumption was carefully computed, together with the maximum number of hours which the known petrol capacity it could be hoped to maintain flight.'

A drift indicator, a Reid Turn indicator, was fitted and the aircraft compass – the type used by the RAF – was swung and the variations carefully logged. Like many aviators both before and after him, Captain Hinchliffe decided not to take a wireless on the perilous journey, though this may initially appear foolish to the point of negligent. He believed that the presence of petrol fumes in the plane would make it much too risky because an electrical spark could blow the plane apart, perhaps even before take-off; in any case, every single inch of space was needed for the fuel supply so there simply wasn't room. Besides, a wireless was of questionable use; radio technology was still fairly primitive and those aviators who chose to take them found them little help in times of crisis, dependent as they were on a ship being in the vicinity and the crew accurately knowing their position.

In September 1927 another Stinson Detroiter called *Sir John Carling* – after the name of the sponsoring brewery – was part of a cross-Atlantic race from London, Ontario, to London, England. Despite carrying a radio, the plane and crew were lost without trace. At the same time the flight of *Old Glory*, sponsored by newspaper tycoon William Randolph Hearst, took off carrying the finest radio equipment then available. The following day the plane was beyond the reach of land stations but at least four ocean liners in the mid-Atlantic began to pick up SOS signals. The plane was clearly in trouble. Several ships raced to the radioed position but there was no sign of the plane. Six days later, wreckage was found some five hundred miles off the coast of Newfoundland more than a hundred miles from the spot the crew had given as part of their distress signal. Despite the fact that the plane had also carried a rubber raft, signal flares and rockets, the three crew were never found.

Elsie and Captain Hinchliffe with the *Endeavour*.
(photograph courtesy of Random House)

Captain Hinchliffe took precautions against the possibility of ice forming on the outer fabric of the plane by coating the fuselage and wings with paraffin. The *Endeavour*, like many aeroplanes of the period, was covered in fabric stretched tightly across the frame to form a skin and covered with a medium called 'dope' – a plasticised lacquer used to tighten, stiffen and waterproof the fabric. Emilie Hinchliffe later wrote that: 'In short every possible emergency was foreseen and as far as humanly ascertainable, guarded against.'

With these actions completed, all that was left were the full load and endurance tests but another problem arose that had faced those who had previously tackled long-distance flights: the issue of finding a runway long enough to allow a fully loaded plane to take off.

Aviation historian Quentin Wilson, who has studied the Hinchliffe and Mackay flight for many years, explained that, using the details published in the autumn 1928 edition of the *RAF Cadet College Magazine*, he calculated that the *Endeavour* would have had an approximate take-off weight of 5809lbs, well above the manufacturer's maximum of 3800lbs. He concluded that this 'would have reduced the ability of the aircraft to accelerate resulting in a much longer than normal take-off run.'

Although there were a number of airfields in the UK at that time Captain Hinchliffe decided, as a result of his own calculations, that only one had the sufficient length of runway for such a plane to take off fully loaded. Gaining permission to use that airfield was another matter.

The RAF aerodrome and college at Cranwell near Grantham in Lincolnshire had the necessary length of runway and Hinch had been stationed there as an instructor during the war. However, during his association with Charles Levine the American's staff had caused considerable trouble; as a result, RAF command had taken the decision that civilians would never be allowed to use the base again. The Honourable Elsie Mackay drew on her top-level connections and her powers of persuasion to gain a meeting with the Secretary of State for Air, Sir Samuel Hoare. Her meeting was successful – to a point. They were given permission to use the base but only for a limited period: one week. It gave them a small window to work with and increased their optimism that the stars were on their side.

The modified Stinson Detroiter had now been customised in distinctive black paint picked out with gold on the struts and wires; this design was part of Elsie's input to the preparations. It had a large letter G on the side to signify Great Britain and sported two Union Jacks on the fuselage, together with the name *Endeavour*. The aircraft, serial number 223, also showed an incorrect registration number X41831, its real number being X4183.

On February 24th the plane was flown to Cranwell from Brooklands with Captain Hinchliffe in his usual right-hand seat and Elsie Mackay next to him in the cockpit. Their arrival in Lincolnshire sparked considerable, and unwanted, interest from the local and national press, who started asking questions. The duo were prepared and had a cover story planned, so the eager reporters were told that Captain Hinchliffe was preparing to attempt a long-distance record by flying non-stop to India and Miss Mackay had a small financial interest in the project. An old friend of Captain Hinchliffe's, Captain Gordon Sinclair, would be the co-pilot on the India venture.

When Elsie's continued presence in the cockpit was noticed, Hinch answered the inevitable questions with: 'My assistant pilot has been taken ill and an operation necessary (sic). And Miss Mackay, who is a pilot and who is interested in the project took part in the preliminary flights to see that the engine was working properly.' But just at this point the known weather over the Atlantic deteriorated and the planned take-off had to be delayed.

Although many would later question the wisdom of planning a flight in late February, Elsie chose the time because her parents were abroad. Lord and Lady Inchcape were in Egypt on a lengthy visit to enable Lady Inchcape to recuperate from recent poor health. But with Lord Inchcape's extensive government connections it was only a matter of time before news of Elsie's presence at Cranwell and interest in the project would find its way to them, even though they were in North Africa.

After months of careful preparations carried out in utmost secrecy, and with everything ready for take-off, the whole project was suddenly blown wide open. On the 7th March, Captain Hinchliffe's American agent, believing the departure was imminent, released the news that his client was indeed planning an attempt on the east to west Atlantic route. In the United Kingdom *The Daily Express* seized on the revelation with all the satisfaction of someone who had believed this to be the case all along, and they added the claim that the Honourable Elsie Mackay would accompany the famous pilot to their story. Elsie was furious. The plane was grounded due to the worst March weather to hit the country for years and now there was every chance that, after all the lengths she'd gone to keep everything hush hush, her father would learn of her plans. She immediately denied any involvement in the venture other than sponsorship and personally telephoned the editor of *The Daily Express* to threaten legal action unless the report was retracted.

In order to throw everyone off the scent, Elsie made a big show of attending a prestigious royal event in London on behalf of P&O. At the official send-off ceremony for Princess Mary and Viscount Lascelles at Victoria Station, Elsie told the correspondent of *The New York Times*: 'The report that I am to fly with Captain Hinchliffe is entirely incorrect. I have been flying with him at Cranwell because I have a financial interest in his flight. He is going to cross the Atlantic but not till after a non-stop flight to India.'

In a separate interview, Elsie told a reporter: 'It is quite true that I have been up in every test flight of the machine including a seven hour test with Captain Hinchliffe. It is also true that I have helped to finance the venture and I would give anything to go on the Atlantic trip but two things stop me from going – Captain Hinchliffe is a woman hater in the air, and the opposition of my father.'

On March 9th, *The Daily Express* claimed that the secret plan to fly the Atlantic had been abandoned due to 'premature publicity' and quoted a statement to that effect made to *The New York Evening Sun* by Captain Hinchliffe's American manager, John Gillespie. Unable to gain access to Captain Hinchliffe, reporters approached Emilie for a quote but she had been well briefed by her husband and said: 'Miss Mackay will not go with him. He will take Gordon Sinclair, a former Royal Air Force pilot, on the India flight and his companion across the Atlantic is still undecided.'

An article in *The New York Times* reported that the plane was now closely guarded and no civilians were allowed onto the airfield but it was known that tests continued and there were reports of the machine being flown for twenty-four hours 'droning around the surrounding countryside'.

The Sydney Sun newspaper regarded the whole thing as a comedy in contrast to the usual tragedy that accompanied long-distance flying. Claiming that the 'secret was out', the report stated that, following the revelation from Hinchliffe's US agent, 'London reporters in a fleet of swift motor cars reached the aerodrome' where there was 'in the hanger, with tanks filled to the brim and fully provisioned, the Stinson monoplane obviously ready for long range action.'

Unable to gain access to the aerodrome, and with the reporters still trying to get to the bottom of the mystery by questioning local villagers, news came of another cable from the US agent stating that 'it was true that Captain Hinchliffe and Elsie Mackay had secretly arranged to fly to New York but premature publicity had forced them to abandon the flight.' The *Sun's* special representative claimed that the 'force' had come in the form of a 'phone talk which a surprised and irate peer had with his adventurous daughter after reading his newspaper at breakfast'. It can only be assumed, given the statements that were issued later, that Elsie repeated her assurances that her only interest in the flight was as a sponsor, dismissing the newspaper claims as nonsense and hoping the retraction of the report would allay her father's fears.

Pressure was building. The threat of legal action temporarily gagged the papers but journalists now knew that some kind of long-distance record-breaking flight was being planned by the famous pilot, and an irate editor was keen to prove that his hunch had been correct. Reporters were unable to get into Cranwell but they kept a close watch everywhere else. Lord Inchcape's suspicions had been aroused and he set in motion enquiries to ascertain what his daughter was really up to.

The obvious move for Hinchliffe and Mackay was to set off at the earliest opportunity. Everything was ready, every test had been done, every inch of the *Endeavour* checked and double checked, every foreseeable problem had been prepared for as much as it was humanly possible – but the one thing that could not be predicted or guarded against was the British weather. Unseasonable snow threatened to ruin the months of preparation and secrecy. The weather was unusually bad even for March and it caused continuing, frustrating delays. *The Ayrshire Post* commented that 'exceptionally severe weather' had been felt on both sides of the Atlantic: 'The snowstorm which swept over England and Scotland was of almost unprecedented severity for the season of the year. In most districts snow fell very heavily and occasioned considerable inconvenience to traffic, while Arctic conditions generally were directly responsible for a number of fatal accidents.' *The Glasgow Herald* featured photographs of the city in deep snow and reported, at length, on the chaos created throughout the country by the 'worst March weather for many years.'

Whilst the weather was a severe hazard for everyone in the country, at The George Hotel in Lincolnshire it was the source of the most intense frustration for two particular people. It was impossible to take off and pressure was mounting. Hinchliffe and Mackay had already exceeded the time limit agreed by Sir Samuel Hoare, Minister for Air; on top of that, the mistake by the American agent meant that press reporters were closing in on the truth.

Elsie feared that if her father had not been convinced by her claim that she would not be flying with Hinchliffe then he would bring pressure to bear to prevent her from flying – even from Egypt. Such was Elsie's confidence in her success that she believed that by flying secretly she would prevent unnecessary distress to her ailing mother, who had recently suffered problems resulting from a heart condition. Her parents were staying at Helouan, about twenty miles from Cairo, for Lady Inchcape to recuperate in a more favourable climate. So sure was Elsie that the crossing would succeed that she planned to reveal her presence on the flight from the safety of New York after it was completed.

The captain and Miss Mackay kept up their policy of misinformation in the hope that it would mislead the press and anyone reading the daily papers. Captain Hinchliffe continued with the line that his friend Captain Sinclair would be accompanying him on an overland flight. He told reporters: 'Miss Mackay is one of the pluckiest women I have known. No pilot could wish to have a more efficient or reliable assistant, I only wish she could come. Unfortunately it was found impossible for a woman to take part in the flight. Each can of petrol weighs some 70 lbs and it would be impossible for a woman to handle them in order to feed the fuel tanks. The machine is only a two seater so Miss Mackay cannot be carried as a passenger.' Of course Elsie had been trained in all aspects of the flight for months and Emilie Hinchliffe would later reveal that the Stinson Detroiter had been chosen partly because of the dual controls, which would enable her to fly the plane while Captain Hinchliffe dealt with the fuel.

In an interview with *The Daily Express*, Captain Hinchliffe confirmed that his intention was to make his mark in aviation. He told the paper's air correspondent: 'It has long been my wish to make a record-breaking flight for Great Britain.' He confirmed that because of Captain Sinclair's absence, Miss Mackay had been helping with preliminary test flights to ensure that the engine was working correctly. 'The failure of my flight with Mr Levine was due to the fact that the petrol pumps broke down three times. This time we are determined to take no risk.' He told the journalist that although he intended taking a long-distance flight over land, or to make an attempt on the endurance record by circling the aerodrome: 'I shall try to be the first man to reach America by air though the exact date depends on weather conditions and the time by which the airplane is fit to start.'

Friday March 9th had been set as their departure date but a hail storm raged and the weather deteriorated even further. The flyers, together with Captain Sinclair, were forced to wait it out at their unofficial headquarters at the hotel. Heavy snow hindered any plans for take-off and there was nothing they could do. Emilie Hinchliffe had been with her husband for the Friday take-off but they agreed that she should go home for the weekend and return on the following Tuesday.

Elsie had the companionship of her friend Sophie Ries, though some reporters later claimed she was a maid called Rees; they had booked into the hotel on February 25th with only Sophie signing the register. At times the women returned to London in the evening but always returned to the airfield first thing the following morning. But, as the hours of that final weekend passed, it was becoming clear that Elsie's father remained suspicious and a cable arrived at the hotel addressed to Elsie under her own name.

According to Ralph Barker, the author of *Great Mysteries of the Air*, Lord Inchcape wired his son Viscount Glenapp and asked him to find out if there was any truth in the story that Elsie was involved in a long-distance flight, possibly over the Atlantic.

To add to the pilots' miseries another telegram arrived, this time from the Air Ministry, reminding them that their agreement had expired and instructing them that the *Endeavour* should be moved from RAF Cranwell forthwith. Knowing that Lord Inchcape had gleaned that something was afoot, it is impossible not to speculate that his influence played a part in this ultimatum. Lord Inchcape moved in the highest government circles and knew the minister, Sir Samuel Hoare, socially.

Tragically, in what may have been a move to foil or further delay the flight, this pressure added to Hinchliffe and Elsie taking an even bigger risk. Elsie was shocked and surprised by the unexpected arrival of her brother Kenneth and brother-in-law Alexander Shaw. Elsie was very close to her brother and if anyone could get to the bottom of what she was planning, it was him. What discussions and arguments passed between them was never made public but from later statements issued by the family it can be assumed that she gave assurances that her interest in the adventure was purely as a sponsor.

At that point, there was a massive question mark hanging over the whole project. The weather delay and the telegram from the Air Ministry must have made Elsie wonder if the flight would go ahead at all. There was also every chance that she would change her mind at the last minute and allow Captain Sinclair to go in her stead. Her assurances to her family may have been a tad disingenuous but her thoughts at that time would have been mixed and troubled. Problem piled on top of problem and, if things were not bad enough, further unwelcome news arrived at the hotel: a German attempt on the east-west route in the well-tested Junkers monoplane, the *Bremen*, piloted by Captain H. Koehl and Baron Von Huenefeld, was rumoured to be about to set off from Berlin.

German aviators had been inspired by the achievement and subsequent publicity tour by Chamberlin and Levine the previous year. The *Bremen*, with pilots Koehl, Frederick Loose and the Baron, was one of two planes involved in an east to west race in August 1927. Taking off from Dessau the second plane, the *Europa*, was first to turn back due to poor visibility but the Bremen passed over Ireland and flew 1800 miles before also reluctantly returning to land and safety. This double failure was a bitter blow to air enthusiasts in Germany who were keen to get the country's aviation industry back on its feet following defeat in the war and the subsequent restrictions of the Versailles Treaty. The airmen had learned the lesson that the potency of the headwinds and the impact of the weather, especially fog, was critical on the east to west route.

The genteel surroundings of The George Hotel must have felt like a pressure cooker during that snow-bound weekend but Hinchliffe and Mackay, together with Captain Sinclair, continued to pore over maps and discuss routes. When Monday dawned, the daily weather chart showed little improvement and their time had run out. A second urgent telegram arrived from the Air Ministry informing them that the *Endeavour* must be moved from RAF Cranwell by the following day at the latest.

Considering their limited options Elsie and Hinch faced two choices: either make the attempt or fly the plane back to Brooklands. With the Germans hot on their heels, no guarantee that they would be given permission to use Cranwell again, and with Elsie's family clearly suspicious of her involvement, moving the *Endeavour* was essentially an admission of defeat. Even if the German flight failed and permission to use the airfield could be gained again, there would be no chance for Elsie to be on board the plane – that small window of opportunity was closing.

Captain Hinchliffe's friend John T. Cummings later revealed that he received a letter in which the airman wrote of the need to make the Atlantic flight as soon as possible. 'He said that if he didn't go soon someone else would and that after the first man made it "there would be a steady stream of planes to follow suit".'

The Daily Express claimed that Captain Hinchliffe stated on the day before leaving: 'They say March is too early in the year to attempt a transatlantic flight. My reply is that it is too late. During my delay I have discovered that there are 12 expeditions awaiting the word go. I shall get the record for this country or...'.

Image of Hinch and Elsie in flying gear.
(photograph courtesy of Laurie Notaro)

On Monday evening, the trio of flyers clandestinely visited the Grantham Picture House as the manager had given them permission to use the cinema to screen footage that had been taken of the Endeavour. They wanted to study how she handled as she took off from the snowy Cranwell runway. The three of them sat in the otherwise empty auditorium studying the flickering film of the small plane rumbling along the runway and heaving itself into the air. A number of companies that had heard of the proposed long-distance flight sent products for the aviators to use including Sidcot suits (special flying overalls), and a caterer supplied food in a 'concentrated form' and fresh sandwiches each night in case the flight went ahead the next morning.

Back at the hotel Elsie ordered flasks of soup, tea and coffee. Sandwiches had been standard fare for distance flyers following a fashion set by Alcock and Brown who, on their successful 1919 Atlantic crossing, had taken coffee, chocolate and sandwiches. In 1934 when Beryl Markham became the first woman to fly solo from east to west she took similar provisions: a packet of chicken sandwiches, a chewing mixture of nuts, raisins and dried banana, five flasks of tea and coffee, a hip flask of brandy and a bottle of water.

After discussions into the early hours, followed by restless sleep, decisions had to be made. Elsie spent the night wrestling with her conscience, weighing up her burning ambition with thoughts of her father, the delicacy of her mother's health and the words she had exchanged with her brother. The Cairo correspondent of the news agency Reuter later revealed that Lord Inchcape sent an urgent eleventh-hour telegram to his daughter appealing to her not to go.

Elsie was all too aware of the risks she was taking and, after collecting her flying suit and goggles, gloves and helmet, she made her way to the church of St Mary Immaculate at North Parade in Grantham. Swathed in a scarf in the hope of disguising her appearance from any waiting reporters, she left the hotel; only the night porter, who later revealed that he noticed flying breeches beneath her fur coat, witnessed her departure. *The Ayr Advertiser* later reported that 'at five o'clock in the darkness that precedes the dawn' Elsie took Holy Communion with the local priest at the dimly lit alter. Elsie had converted to the Roman Catholic faith only a few months before in December 1927. She had attended the service on the previous Sunday morning with Sophie Ries, and had visited again on Monday evening for the priest, Father Arendzen, to hear her confession.

When Elsie rang the bell of the rectory at 5am on Tuesday morning, she was wearing her full flying kit and carrying her helmet and a small leather bag. After receiving communion and the priest's blessing, she knelt in prayer for a long time under the great crucifix that hung over the sanctuary. 'This young and valiant woman was deeply conscious of the great hazard on which she was setting out,' reported *The Angus Evening Telegraph*.

Eventually she accompanied the priest back to his study, where she revealed the secret of her trip. 'I hoped she would fare better than Princess Ludwig of Lowenstein-Wertheim,' Father Arendzen later told reporters. 'She was obviously excited and was deeply affected by the step she was taking. She was a strong-minded, courageous woman and seemed to have the faith of a simple girl. One recalled the soldiers at Communion on the night before a battle. We both knelt for a long time in prayer. I essayed to advise her and Miss Mackay seemed once or twice on the verge of tears but her only retort was a courageous smile. With a wave of her hand she left me for the unknown.'

As Captain Hinchliffe arrived at RAF Cranwell an officer gave him the latest weather reports, which showed a rare easterly wind; it seemed like a positive omen to a man who had always been superstitious about the number thirteen, and Tuesday was the 13th of March. In the *Endeavour's* log book the captain wrote what would be his final entry: 'My confidence in the success of the venture is now 100%.' His wife later commented that 'we, who loved him, were equally confident. The remotest possibility of failure occurred to none of us.'

Elsie remained in her car until Captain Hinchliffe went over to share the results of the weather report. He said: 'Everything is ready now. The report seems good and we have an east wind here.' They were observed speaking quietly to each other for a few minutes and then the deliberations were over. Elsie, now wrapped in layers of warm clothing topped with the Sidcot suit, committed herself to the flight and shook hands with Captain Sinclair, leaving him to play his next role – that of decoy.

A final photograph was taken of the flyers and published in *The Daily Express*. The petite Elsie Mackay is almost unrecognisable in her flying gear as she smiles bravely at the camera. She and Captain Hinchliffe stand in front of the *Endeavour* and the brightness of the snow makes the image look almost like a negative.

A small gathering of two RAF officers, an American mechanic, Elsie's chauffeur and Captain Sinclair watched the flyers climb into the cockpit of the Detroiter. Captain Hinchliffe had spoken briefly with the mechanic and Sinclair saying that if things were not good he would land at Baldonnel, otherwise 'it is straight on.' Only Captain Sinclair and the mechanic knew for certain that the pilots were not simply moving the aircraft or heading east towards India but would be turning west in an attempt to cross the Atlantic.

At 8.35am on Tuesday March 13th 1928, Captain Hinchliffe saw the propeller swing and heard the Wright Whirlwind engine roar into life. Captain Sinclair later told *The Manchester Guardian*: 'The *Endeavour* was wheeled round in readiness to take off. The engines were started up and Captain Hinchliffe climbed aboard with his passenger, and that was the last I saw of them. Everything was in readiness for the flight. I shook them both by the hand, wished them good luck.' But the take-off was the first of the many challenges to come and the long grass runway at RAF Cranwell was still covered in snow.

Experienced pilots knew that the first few minutes of a long-distance flight were amongst the most dangerous a flyer would face. It was not a certainty that a heavily overloaded plane would get off the ground, even with a mile-long runway. One mistake and the little aeroplane, which was really no more than a giant flying petrol tank, could end up as a fireball before leaving the ground.

Aviation historian Quentin Wilson calculated that on take-off the *Endeavour* was loaded to over fifty per cent above the maximum design weight for the aircraft. 'This would have reduced the ability of the aircraft to accelerate resulting in a much longer than normal take-off run and a slower rate of climb once off the ground. Overloading the aircraft by over fifty per cent was potentially very dangerous since the safety margins on the structure would have been of a similar order, risking structural failure of the fully fuelled *Endeavour* at the very beginning of the attempt on the Atlantic crossing.'

Getting the plane off the ground was not the end of the danger for these flights as author C. St John Spriggs wrote at the time: 'Suppose the engine splutters and stops now? If the pilot attempts to turn back, the aeroplane will certainly stall and spin. His only chance is to land on whatever is ahead of him – houses, fields or roads, knowing all the time that his aeroplane is loaded with the makings of a blazing inferno.'

The last image of the *Endeavour* as it prepared for take-off.
(photograph courtesy of Laurie Notaro)

But, with a roar of the engine, the *Endeavour* taxied across the snow-covered ground to the far side of the airfield before building up speed and finally lifting into the air, then almost disappearing into the mist. In a minute the monoplane returned, dipping slightly as if to bid farewell to the little group of officials and civilians below before flying out of sight. Captain Sinclair said: 'The next thing I can remember was waving cheerily to the Endeavour as it became a smaller and smaller spot on the horizon.' Another 'eyewitness' of what was at first reported as a 'mystery flight' told *The Manchester Guardian*: 'I don't think anyone was expecting a start would be made. The conditions were very wintry, snow covered the ground as far as one could see. Captain Hinchliffe did not say where he was going but after flying conditions were ascertained and the final preparations made the pair took their places in the machine and set off towards the west. The plane, which was carrying a heavy load of petrol, ran a great distance along the ground leaving its tracks in the snow, before it soared into the air.'

What was described in *The Daily Express* as 'the most secret flight in the history of aviation' took to the skies heading for Ireland and the 1900 miles of icy depths beyond. As Captain Hinchliffe set the course, notification of their take-off was officially sent through to the Air Ministry although the destination was still not made public.

As part of his promise to Miss Mackay, Captain Sinclair quietly slipped from the airfield into hiding, a deliberate move that would cause much confusion and speculation over the following days. At one point his very existence was called into question by reporters. One eyewitness claimed that 'the passenger in the machine was definitely Mr Gordon Sinclair' but, of course, this witness could have been the captain himself trying to throw the newshounds off the scent.

Frenzied speculation about who was in the cockpit dominated the headlines as journalists got wind that Captain Hinchliffe was not simply on another test flight. 'Hinchliffe Takes Off for America with Daughter of Lord Inchcape: passes Ireland and heads out to sea', announced *The New York Times*. *The Manchester Guardian* asked: 'Atlantic Flight in Progress; Captain Hincliffe's Secret Start on Westward Attempt; Peer's Daughter as Passenger?' *The Glasgow Herald* raised a different question: 'Who is Mr Sinclair's Passenger's Identity Puzzle', reporting that Captain Hinchliffe had left a message with a London evening newspaper stating that he 'was starting out from Cranwell on an attempt to fly the Atlantic.'

Hopes were high for their success as reports came in that the *Endeavour* had been spotted by Civil Guards at the Kilmeaden Barracks on the western border of County Waterford 'flying very fast at high altitude' at 11.30am. *The Manchester Guardian* commented that the plane had flown 280 miles in two hours and fifty minutes, 'a remarkable pace considering the load the plane was carrying.' A further report carried in the same newspaper stated that

Commandant Fitzmaurice, whose name would shortly be associated with the *Bremen* flight, had relayed the news that the lighthouse keeper at Mizen Head in County Cork at the southernmost tip of Ireland had seen a plane pass over at 1.30pm. The coastguard at Crook Haven, in the same area, confirmed the sighting. *The Manchester Guardian* also reported that the weather was bad, with heavy snow and sleet falling with an adverse wind. A ship 170 miles off the Irish coast later reported seeing a small plane. According to *The Glasgow Herald*: 'a wireless message intercepted at New York apparently relayed by the *Roussillon* from another steamer which was four days out of Bordeaux reports the vessel passed a large plane low overhead heading west.'

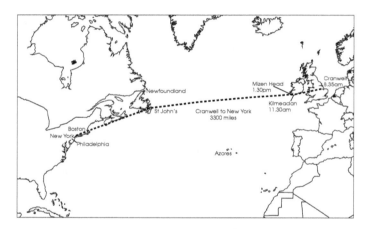

Aviation experts believed Hinchliffe and Mackay would follow
the Great Circle Route across the Atlantic.

It was widely thought that Captain Hinchliffe had avoided announcing any landing place because of the unknown conditions surrounding a successful westward Atlantic flight that might necessitate deviations from the original plan but 'if he lands anywhere in the United States he will receive a hero's welcome,' *The Daily Express* claimed.

Newspapers on both sides of the Atlantic continued to speculate as to who was really in the co-pilot's seat. Some believed that Captain Gordon Sinclair existed in name alone and this had simply been a cover story to disguise the identity of the real pilot, the Honourable Elsie Mackay. The story was fuelled by the disappearance of the mysterious captain who, on Elsie's instructions, had gone to ground in the hope that her part would only be revealed by her safe and triumphant arrival in Philadelphia.

John Gillespie, Hinchliffe's New York agent, told the press the aviators' intentions were not definite but if fuel allowed they would attempt to reach Philadelphia in order to win a $25,000 prize that was on offer to the first flyer from Europe. This aim would mean flying a further one thousand miles on top of the basic distance of 2300 miles from RAF Cranwell to Newfoundland. Chamberlain and Levine had flown non-stop for 3905 miles in thirty-six hours and Lindbergh 3610 miles in thirty-three hours but both flights were blown along with the prevailing winds during the summer season. Trying to fly that distance against those winds in snow and sleet during March was a completely different matter.

Captain Hinchliffe's English agent, Harvey Lloyd, appeared to be perplexed by his client's actions. A note had been sent to him 'written by someone other than his client' that simply read 'leaving on Atlantic attempt' and he told reporters that he 'was as much at sea about this as most people. I saw Captain Hinchliffe on Friday. He said to me then: "I don't see any opportunity of doing the long-distance flight until we get a full moon." I had a telegram this morning to say that Captain Hinchliffe had left at 8.45am as he had been asked by the Air Ministry to leave Cranwell for another aerodrome. I thought that was what he had done.' Mr Lloyd added that he had travelled to Grantham to try and gain some information for himself and he had also made 'endless enquiries in London' but had learned very little apart from the mysterious note.

The suddenness of the departure clearly surprised everyone, even those who were in on the secret. Emilie Hinchliffe told the correspondent of *The New York Times*: 'You may not believe me but I did not know until lunch time today (the 13th) that he was on his way across the ocean. I knew this morning that he left Cranwell but I thought he was simply going to Ireland on a short flight.' From conversations she had had with her husband, she assumed that his destination would be Mitchell Field, Long Island. Emilie added that she had every confidence in her husband's success: 'he is a wonderful flier and he knows his business.' She claimed that Captain Sinclair's wife didn't know where he was though they had agreed that both the captain and Miss Mackay could not both be on board the plane. 'It seems such a waste of petrol carrying space; I really don't know,' she said. 'The *Endeavour* has dual controls and my husband has high opinion of her as a pilot.'

The surprise and confusion about the flight and who was in the cockpit were increased by the reaction of the staff at the Inchcape's London residence at Seamore Place. Although Elsie had been at The George Hotel on Monday night, a *Daily Express* reporter was informed that: 'Miss Mackay left here at half-past eight this morning (13th) and she said that if she was not back at teatime she would not be home until very late. She has not left London. We have heard the rumour that Miss Mackay has gone with Captain Hinchliffe on his transatlantic flight but there cannot be any truth in it. Miss Mackay has been busy recently preparing for a journey to Egypt where she is to join Lord Inchcape next week.' A further statement claimed that 'Miss Mackay left the house this morning saying she would be returning sometime this evening. We believe she spent the day in London.'

Despite these claims, the conclusion that the media and the public were coming to was that it was indeed the Honourable Elsie Mackay who had taken the second seat in the cockpit, a conclusion that appeared to be confirmed by a statement quoted widely the following day by the *Central News Agency* that came from an 'unnamed close relative of Lord Inchcape'. It read that he had said that he had every reason to believe that the supposition was correct: 'I am afraid to say "No" and it is a matter of grave anxiety to us.'

Members of Elsie's family had clearly had to turn detective to get to the bottom of the elaborate plans she had drawn up to keep them in the dark. *The Daily Mail* reported that after reading of Elsie's association with the captain a 'close relative' became anxious and made enquiries about her whereabouts. She was initially told by servants at Seamore Place that Elsie had not left home until after eight o'clock that morning (March 13th) but when the relative continued with her enquiries, she finally learned that Elsie had in fact secretly left the Mayfair house the day before. It is, perhaps, an indication of the love and loyalty the staff felt towards Elsie that they stuck to the story she had asked them to give not only to the persistent reporters but also to other members of the family.

In London on the day following the take-off Lord Inchcape's eldest daughter, Mrs Alexander Shaw, told the papers that 'Elsie had promised definitely not to go on the flight with Hinchliffe and of course we never dreamed she would do so. There is no doubt, however, that she is gone.' She confirmed that Miss Mackay had not left a message and the only information they had was from the newspapers. The close family had stayed up all night hoping to hear some good news but no definite news had come, only false hopes.

Following the dramatic take-off *The Daily Express* was keen to confirm its scoop from the week before, the scoop so vehemently denied by Elsie, that the beautiful heiress was in the cockpit and that the pilots' destination was America. The news editor immediately instigated a search for Miss Mackay: 'The evasive replies of those connected with the flight and the inability to find Miss Mackay resulted in final confirmation of the fact that she had gone,' the paper told its readers. In Scotland *The Glasgow Herald* revealed that both aviators had recently obtained visas for their passports from the American Consul in preparation for the flight, providing a strong clue to the family and public that this attempt had been planned for some time.

Captain Hinchliffe's parents talked about their opposition to their son's flying ambitions during a visit to RAF Cranwell the previous year when he was working with Charles Levine. At that time his mother told the press: 'We are against such adventurous undertakings of this kind and argued against it or any others from the start but without result. Walter had his heart set on making a non-stop record and all our pleadings had not the slightest effect.'

The truth behind the identity of Captain Hinchliffe's co-pilot was finally and dramatically established by the press when Captain Sinclair, described as the 'most sought after man in the British Isles during the last 36 hours', emerged from hiding. He revealed his whereabouts by arriving at the Hinchliffe family home, a house called Hoekhuis in Peak's Hill, Purley, to join his wife, who had travelled there to be with Emilie Hinchliffe. Interviewed by *The Daily Mail*, he admitted he had been involved in the preparations for the flight and had hoped to be in the cockpit with his friend. He explained that it had initially been Miss Mackay's intention to fly as far as Baldonnel aerodrome in Ireland but, finding the weather conditions favourable, they must have decided to make 'a dash across the Atlantic.' His friend had told him many times that if the conditions were favourable he would not land at Newfoundland but 'push on to Philadelphia.'

He explained that Miss Mackay would either fly the machine or help transfer the petrol to the main tanks. 'She did not seem at all anxious about the outcome of the adventure. She was smiling as the machine took into the air.' Captain Sinclair also provided an explanation for his disappearance, saying that he had promised to keep Miss Mackay's departure a secret. 'I came straight back to London where I have been lying low purely because I wanted to keep my word to Miss Mackay. The only reason she did not want her flight known until it had been safely accomplished was to avoid undue anxiety,' he told reporters. *The Manchester Guardian* reported that the captain claimed that it was only in the last few hours before the flight that Miss Mackay made her final decision to fly. 'All I knew,' he said, 'was that suddenly at two o'clock on Tuesday morning – we stayed up all night busy with our preparations – I was told that I was not going to fly.'

As speculation continued on both sides of the Atlantic, and the whereabouts of the *Endeavour* was unknown, the news reached the south Ayrshire village of Ballantrae that Miss Elsie was involved in a dangerous escapade. Held in high esteem by so many in this small coastal community, the news was initially greeted with excitement but this soon turned to grave concern. *The Ayrshire Post* reported that 'there was a keen wish that they would win through' based on the knowledge that both participants were skilled pilots. Although the story was front-page news in the major cities of the UK and US, the people of Ballantrae had to turn to the district news page and the section featuring their village before they could read about Miss Elsie. The village's correspondent for *The Girvan Town Crier and Pavilion News* wrote: 'During the last few days one topic of conversation in the village has been the Atlantic flight of the Hon. Elsie Mackay. The few facts in connection with Capt Hinchliffe's attempt to fly the Atlantic from east to west are known. Miss Mackay is a favourite in the village and hopes and wishes for her safety are heard on every side.' *The Ayrshire Post* reported that at the opening of a concert and dance for the Laggan United Football Club in the school at Auchenflower 'the anxiety and sympathy felt by the community as to the fate of their neighbour, Miss Elsie Mackay of Glenapp', was expressed.

As international concern grew for the fate of the flyers, the newspapers began to speculate about weather conditions over the Atlantic and the truth behind possible sightings. They believed that favourable conditions had been likely until mid-ocean but there were adverse winds and squally weather near Newfoundland. *The New York Times* reported that that the crews of transatlantic steamers had been watching the skies, believing that that *Endeavour's* most likely path was the Great Circle route. Among the ships were the *Cedric*, which Hinch had been on board only a few months before, and the *Majestic*, a vessel that Elsie had travelled on with her father some years earlier; but there were no sightings.

In New York Ruth Elder, who had been so lucky to survive her own transatlantic attempt, paid tribute to Elsie at a luncheon meeting of the League of Advertising Women held at the Hotel Astor. 'I hope and pray the English girl will make it', she told the 150-strong audience; 'she certainly has fine courage to undertake such a difficult flight, especially on the Northern route, which at this time of year may force her to land in icebound Newfoundland or a worse place.' Revealing the rigours of a transatlantic flight, she spoke of her own experience as being a 'royal battle from beginning to end. I never expect to go through anything as horrible as that again. Every night I say a little prayer of thanks that I'm still alive.'

The New York Times revealed that when he was expecting to fly with Charles Levine, Captain Hinchliffe had written an article for the newspaper that gave a fascinating insight into 'the gallant Englishman's outlook on the adventure which he was to try seven months later on another plane and with another passenger.' The captain had written: 'We are off on a great adventure. The one wish of my long flying career has been to accomplish something which no one else has yet done and my opportunity seems to have come. I am looking forward with keen interest to this flight across the Atlantic. The flight itself so far as I can see is not more difficult than the west to east crossing although we are certain to meet contrary winds most of the way. But this, after all, merely means more hours in the air and provided the commissary department holds out that should not matter much. We have made a careful study of the weather maps and are planning to fly along the great circle course. After taking off from Cranwell we will steer straight across the Atlantic to some central point in Newfoundland. Atmospheric conditions may cause us to take a more southerly course and come down nearer the northern steamer routes but that will all depend on conditions as we find them.'

He went on to describe how he wished to leave Cranwell at daybreak in order to reach Newfoundland at about dawn the following day, therefore spending just one night over the middle of the Atlantic. He intended to fly low the whole time to take advantage of the greater lift and the lower wind velocities near the sea's surface. 'Another reason for flying low,' he wrote, 'is that much engine power consequently much gasoline is required to attain altitude with loss of speed and we want to conserve every ounce of fuel. Our course has been mapped out and the distance divided into three legs each of which represents three hours flying. At the end of each three hours our magnetic course will be changed to allow for differences in the magnetic variations of that area. By this method the shortest possible water route will be followed. We hope to be able to accomplish this flight which takes the fastest ships five and a half days, in about forty hours. The accomplishment of such a feat certainly brings home strongly the progressiveness of man's inventive genius. I trust that in the very near future we will see the establishment of an air service between England and America.'

As he expected not to reach New York until after nightfall he asked American aviators, on hearing news of their approach, to fly to escort their arrival and people on the ground to burn flares to help them stay on course.

Despite his exhaustive preparations, the reality of the weather conditions over the Atlantic remained a mystery even to the most advanced meteorological scientists and there were some things that simply could not be prepared for. British aviator Beryl Markham described her 1936 successful east–west solo flight in her book *West With the Night*, written in 1942. She flew in September but descriptions of the appalling weather she faced give an insight into the conditions that were, in all likelihood, endured by Hinchliffe and Mackay. 'It was a great adventure,' she wrote. 'But I'm so glad it's over. I really had a terrible time. That's the only word for it – terrible. I knew I was in for it half an hour after I left. There was nothing on the chart but water. There was a 30 mile headwind, a helluva lot of low cloud and driving rain. I almost wanted to turn back. Once I got over the Atlantic I could see nothing but water, and not much of that. Then an electrical storm popped up to make it all gay and happy. But you know I really welcomed that storm, it was a relief to see something besides cloud and water. I was flying at about 2000 feet. I wanted to fly lower so that I could keep an eye on the water but bucking winds made that too dangerous. I passed out of the storm but only into more dirty weather. Once, poor old *Messenger* [the name of Miss Markham's plane] took a terrific toss. I didn't know quite what was happening but she seemed to be behaving in an extraordinary manner. Next time the lightning flashed I took a look out of the window. I was flying upside down. That was a nasty shock. I got so fed up seeing the sea that I said to myself aloud if you don't see something besides water you'll go crazy. I thought about all sorts of things.

'*Messenger* should do about 158 mph cruising speed in still air but I reckoned I was doing about 90. Those nasty old headwinds were to blame for that. I got so weary of battling against the icy gale all the way over that I was just about ready to give up whenever I let myself think about it. I never completely lost my bearings but it seemed so impossible to go on, driving the ship against all odds, knowing that all the time I was using up far more petrol than I thought. I know I got into a spin more than once. I just went on, on, on hoping for the best but not expecting it, bumping and rocking all over the place. I wouldn't have imagined that there was an expanse of desolation so big in the whole world as the waste of sky and water I saw go past me from the time I left Abingdon. It was fog, rain, sleet for hours on end. If I climbed it was sleet, if I dropped it was rain. If I skimmed the sea it was fog. I couldn't see anything beyond my wingtips.'

What Hinchliffe and Mackay were facing could only be guessed at, given the ice and snow in which they had taken off. But as those early reports came in, and as Elsie's presence in the cockpit was confirmed, it was clear that the great adventure was afoot and hopes were high for their success. The intrepid pair were somewhere in the sky over the Atlantic facing wind and weather that would battle with them to throw their little plane off course. Flying westward in March meant that they would spend many hours travelling in darkness, making it impossible to use the waves as a guide to wind speed or direction.

Emilie Hinchliffe and her daughter Joan waiting for news.
(photograph courtesy of Laurie Notaro)

As the Hinchliffe and Inchcape families waited for further news Miss Mackay's car, accompanied by two chauffeurs, brought her friend Miss Ries back to London with her luggage and the two little dogs she had stroked so fondly before leaving. Another car delivered Captain Hinchliffe's bags to his wife at their home in Purley, Surrey. Emilie faced many hours of waiting, hoping that her husband would return to her.

CHAPTER SIX

Hope Fades

As the hours passed following the dramatic and unexpected take-off and the news filtered out, it seemed as if everyone on both sides of the Atlantic and on the sea itself was watching and waiting. From the grandeur of Glenapp Castle to Seamore Place and the Hinchliffe home in Surrey, where Emilie waited with her little daughter and new baby, there was a sense of hope mixed with fervent prayers for the success of the flight. Almost hourly rumours of a plane being heard or seen brought new hope that Captain W. G. R. Hinchliffe and the Honourable Elsie Mackay would become the first aviators to fly the Atlantic east to west.

Thousands of people gathered at Mitchel Field in Philadelphia, the place widely believed to be the destination. They kept a vigil for hours in the hope of greeting the *Endeavour* and its brave crew. With so many people watching the skies, there were numerous reports of sightings; others believed they had heard a plane overhead. After so many tragedies, everyone wanted to believe that this time the flyers would make it.

A fireman and the engineer of a train in New Brunswick reported that they had seen a plane pass over them shortly after 1am on Wednesday morning. Another sighting from Old Orchard in Maine provided an even stronger rumour that the flight had succeeded. A hotel keeper had telephoned the coastguard to say she had seen a yellowish light on one of the small islands and two people moving around – but an inspection by the coastguard found no sign of either an aeroplane or its crew. Such was the near hysteria about the flight that one report of a plane passing overhead in Halifax, Nova Scotia, was discovered, on investigation, to have simply been the sound of a motor lorry.

Sightings were reported in various parts of Newfoundland and at other points along the eastern seaboard but eventually the crowd that had gathered at Mitchel Field, New York's suburban aviation headquarters, began to disperse. Captain Bender, the operations officer, stated that he would keep all the lights going there and at nearby Curtis Field if it was believed that the *Endeavour* was still in the air. Only an hour after the crowds started to leave, a radio station broadcast the news that the plane was due at New York and nearly seven thousand people returned to greet the flyers. At midnight searchlights, including one that shone thirty miles into the sky, and beacons were turned on again and there was a great buzz of expectation. Troops were drafted in to help the police control the huge crowd but eventually, when the *Endeavour* failed to appear, people began to drift away again.

A message from St John's, Newfoundland, received on the Wednesday and quoted in *The Glasgow Herald*, stated: 'It is sunset and still there is no news of Captain Hinchliffe. If he approaches this coast tonight he will find great difficulty in locating Harbour Grace Airfield because the place is unlighted and he will perhaps be forced to descend in the suburbs of St John's, the only area which he is likely to be able to identify. Seafaring opinion here is very dubious on the subject.'

The weather overnight had been clear along the shipping route but there had been no sightings from any liner or from the sealing fleet 150 miles east-north-east of St John's. Further south, the sea coast was shrouded in fog and the coastguard had posted extra lookouts to watch for the *Endeavour*. Captain Hinchliffe had told Captain Sinclair that he 'was confident he would be able to pick out a suitable landing ground near St John's in the dark by the lights of the town if he found it impossible to push on further.'

Numerous reports of planes landing, being spotted or heard in the sky over Boston, New York and Philadelphia all proved to be false alarms. In one case several hundred people in the Boston area reported hearing the sound of a powerful aeroplane heading in the direction of New York. The motor was heard over the East Boston Airport and officials there sent up a score of beacons and flares. Newspaper offices were bombarded with calls from people who thought they'd heard the sound of a Wright Whirlwind engine; others phoned wanting the latest news. George Hamblin, a veteran flyer and Boston correspondent of *The Aero Digest*, was reported as having recognised the 'unmistakeable' sound of the plane passing over his home in Allston, Massachusetts. He did not believe he was mistaken as he knew of only two or three planes with the same engine in New England and he knew that none would be in the air at that time. He strongly believed the plane to be Hinchliffe and Mackay's Stinson Detroiter.

Other reports led to people heading toward their local airfield in such numbers that police had to be drafted to keep order. In other areas the police were kept busy being asked to chase up other sightings. The reporter for The Times said that the rumours of sightings in Newfoundland were not to be trusted as twenty-one ships along the probable course had seen nothing: 'only the faintest belief exists that they have escaped disaster.'

An aviation expert, quoted in the Australian newspaper *The Adelaide Chronicle*, said that Captain Hinchliffe had known 'more than anybody else, the danger of the adventure' but he added, 'if the captain is down in the sea it is not through an error in flying. His experience in fog and mist is unequalled. He must have been beaten by factors over which he had no control. When I reminded Captain Hinchliffe that snow and ice sitting on his wings might force him down he replied, "Yes that's a snag and the one point I have not obtained data. There are none available. If that happens I shall just plod on. Mr Levine told me he was forced down close to the ocean but I don't know. I have left nothing else to chance."'

As speculation continued and the hours passed, further news of just how secret this flight had been began to emerge. Captain Sinclair revealed himself after keeping his promise to Miss Mackay to go to ground. Sophie Ries also spoke to reporters. At first she had remained at The George Hotel, greatly distressed at the possible fate of her friend. 'I was not told by Miss Mackay that she meant to fly the Atlantic,' she revealed, 'she simply told me she was going for an early morning long-distance test and that they might come down at another aerodrome.'

A friend of the Inchcape family, and of Elsie in particular, told one newspaper that events had turned out as she had expected from the moment of the first rumour. 'I have felt all the time that Miss Mackay intended to go and directly I read in last night's paper that Captain Hinchliffe had taken a pilot with him I said to a friend "that is Elsie". She made up her mind I think all the way along to go on this trip and she was particularly annoyed when the news of the flight leaked out last week because she knew that it would make difficulties for her with her people. Lord Inchcape, to whom she is devoted as he is to her, is abroad and we are all terribly anxious. She is a tremendously plucky person and has always had a sense of adventure strongly developed. She had been very keen about flying ever since she was allowed to take it up and she has talked most enthusiastically about this plane. She went up with him a great deal in it and there is this comfort, that she is the last person on earth to lose her head.'

For a brief moment on Thursday afternoon it appeared that the brave flyers had conquered the east-west route. A rumour that they had landed safely at Orchard Beach in Maine flashed from town to town, spreading like wildfire along the east coast so that soon the telephone wires were 'buzzing with excited inquiries about the flyers'. But in the evening the New York radio stations all broadcast religious services for Captain Hinchliffe and Elsie Mackay. Prayers were said and the audiences were urged to join in singing the hymn 'Lead Kindly Light'. *The Glasgow Herald* reported that: 'very sadly and regretfully the American public seems to have come to the conclusion that the transatlantic flight of the golden-winged *Endeavour* which started out so romantically and in the face of such great odds from Cranwell on Tuesday morning, has failed.'

The Scottish reporters remained optimistic, reminding readers that the plane had enough fuel to keep it in the air until 6pm on Wednesday evening and that east-coast airports had remained on alert. Fifty soldiers stayed on duty at Mitchel Field in case crowds returned but gloomy headlines greeted homeward-bound New Yorkers on Wednesday night with 'British Plane Overdue' and 'Fog Veils the Atlantic Coast'.

The American and Canadian governments offered help to send out search parties. The US Secretary of State, Frank B. Kellogg, called the American ambassador in London to say that the navy would 'lend every possible assistance in locating the missing plane' and he expressed the deep anxiety felt in his country for the fate of the 'brave venture.'

The Canadian Minister of Marine, Arthur Cardin, received a telegram from the Pacific Superintendent of the St John Station saying that two lumber men in the woods north of Greenville in Maine were positive they had heard an unknown plane early on Thursday morning. The Canadian Air Force was instructed to conduct a search of the area but many believed that it would be fruitless. *The Manchester Guardian* gloomily reported that the plane seen by the staff on the New Brunswick train was probably a 'rum-running' aircraft and in all likelihood this was the same one spotted by the lumberjacks. A week later a rumour went round the communities in Maine that a Royal Canadian Air Force Observer had seen the wreckage of a plane and two bodies near Island Falls on the Whitecap Mountain but this later proved to be a cruel hoax carried out by local lumber men.

As news of the weather conditions began to come in, it became increasingly clear that the aviators had little chance of success. Ships arriving in port reported a storm in mid-ocean and it was known that the Grand Banks region was notoriously turbulent, with vast ice floes lowering the temperature further and making it almost impossible to keep a plane in the air. *The Adelaide News* reported that: 'wintry squalls or ice forming on the wings of the aeroplane probably brought disaster when the aviators were still several hundred miles off Newfoundland or Labrador or even on an ice pack if their fuel vanished before they could reach land.' There was also the suggestion that the Aurora Borealis, visible over Newfoundland at that time, could have affected the *Endeavour's* compass, throwing the flyers off course, though meteorologists at the Greenwich Observatory felt the disturbance would not have taken the captain far off from his route.

When it became clear that the all the carefully stored fuel must have been spent and the *Endeavour* could no longer be in the air, theories began to be exchanged that a landing on ice was the only remaining possibility for their survival. The Newfoundland correspondent of *The New York Times*, Sir Patrick McGrath, held out some hope as there had been a case just two weeks before of two Canadian government airmen and their Eskimo guide who had been forced down on ice. They had been rescued after reaching safety following an eight-day sixty-mile trek in freezing temperatures. There was a remote possibility that if Hinchliffe and Mackay had landed on an ice pack they could survive long enough to be picked up by the sealing fleet – though they had reported stormy weather and a breaking up of the ice floes in the region.

Newspapers said that because of a lack of definite information the flight of Lord Inchcape's daughter had not been reported to him. When news had leaked out in the week before the flight he had sent an 'urgent appeal to her to refrain from such a perilous undertaking.' When confirmation finally arrived that his daughter had flown with the captain he was 'profoundly affected.' Fearing that the news was too much for his wife, who was in delicate health, he kept it from her. *The Glasgow Herald* told its readers that 'Lord Inchcape therefore while waiting hour by hour for news has been obliged to maintain a courageous mien before his wife, despite his inner anxiety and distress, always hoping that news of his daughter's safety may arrive. The greatest sympathy is manifested in Cairo with Lord Inchcape in the distressing hours through which he is passing.' It was not until it seemed certain that Elsie was lost forever that Lord Inchcape finally told his wife of the terrible secret he had been keeping from her. Biographer Hector Bolitho described Lord Inchcape's actions during those days as being typical of the man. 'The unselfishness and control which would carry him through five days of anxiety without a murmur of open complaint or seeking for sympathy helps one to gauge the nobleness of Lord Inchcape's married life. It was the most engaging characteristic of an ambitious and seemingly unemotional man. He guarded the shrine of his deepest feelings from all eyes.'

It was three days after the take-off on March 16th that Lord Inchcape broke his silence on his daughter's escapade by sending a cablegram from Cairo to the editor of a London evening newspaper. In it he denied any knowledge whatsoever of his daughter's intention to fly the Atlantic. Eighty years later a member of the Mackay family confirmed that his great, great uncle had been unaware that Elsie had gone with Captain Hinchliffe. His grandmother, known to the family as Bluebell, was a cousin of Elsie and being of a similar age they had been very close. In response to a telegram of condolence there was a reply from Lord Inchcape, among her effects, which had been written at the Golf Hotel, Hyeres, in early April. It read: 'My dear Bluebell, I cannot tell you how Aunty Janey and I appreciate your kind telegram. We are extremely grateful for your sympathy in our dreadful trial. Aunt Janey is still bowled over by the shock and won't be equal to the journey home I am afraid for a little time. Elsie had the courage of a lion and at the same time a heart full of tenderness for us and everyone and the end she must have come to in the Atlantic is a continual nightmare. I knew nothing of her intended venture till 36 hours after she had started. I kept it from your Aunty for five days hoping always I would be able to tell her of Elsie's safety. But when hope had vanished I had to break it to her and the shock was dreadful.'

On the day after the sudden take-off Elsie's sister Mrs Alexander Shaw told reporters that 'Elsie had promised definitely not to go on the flight with Hinchliffe and, of course, we never dreamed that she would do so.' On the same day an 'intimate friend of Miss Mackay's in London' confirmed that the preparations for the flight had been going on for months. 'Miss Mackay was delighted with the plane and nothing gave her greater pleasure than to fly with Captain Hinchliffe on its tests. Whenever she returned she was full of enthusiasm at the forthcoming trip across the Atlantic, but she always impressed me with the necessity of absolute secrecy. She was not interested in financial returns but Captain Hinchliffe held the view that it would be remunerative if the attempt were shrouded in mystery.' More than a week had passed after the Endeavour's departure before Sophie Ries issued a statement through the Press Association describing the extent of her distress. 'My pain and anxiety about Miss Mackay, who was a true friend, made it quite impossible for me to bear the thought of interviews. I know nothing at all about the flight except what I read in the newspapers. It was a terrible shock to me to learn that Miss Mackay had gone, for I never dreamt of such a thing. The pain of her loss is very dreadful.'

Journalists reported that Emilie Hinchliffe had been holding on to some hope even as late as Thursday evening. She was pluckily trying to carry on the usual routine of her home and even personally speaking to callers. 'We are still waiting,' she said, 'but there is absolutely no news although we have tried every possible source. We have done everything that could be done to try and get some word.' In Liverpool Captain Hinchliffe's parents were also struggling to sleep for more than an hour at a time, reporters said, but when they managed to rest they were troubled by visions. Revealing a strange psychic trait that would have major ramifications in the ensuing months, the captain's mother claimed that she had received a vision in which she had seen her son flying low over the ocean, turning left when confronted by a huge white cloud. She remained troubled about the fact that her son had taken off on the 13th of March as he had avoided this number all of his life – even refusing to stay in hotel rooms with the number on the door. 'I do not think it is the will of Providence that he should have dropped down in the ocean to his end. He went through the war and suffered a lot and I do not think that Providence means that his end should be in this way. Although things look black we have not given up hope that he is alive,' she said. Her husband said that he had also dreamt about his son, seeing him arrive in America with a woman.

On March 22nd and with rumours and questions rife the Secretary of State for Air, Sir Samuel Hoare, rose in the House of Commons to reply that he had gained further information about the flight. He explained that at the commencement from Cranwell flight officials at the aerodrome telegraphed the Air Ministry in London with the news that no destination had been given by the captain and Miss Mackay but it had been assumed they were heading for an aerodrome in Dublin and no changes had been reported to this. With no positive sightings and all hope slowly slipping away journalists began to consult aviation experts for their opinions on the prospects for the two missing flyers. In France the daily newspaper *Le Matin* speculated on the purpose of such a flight. French airmen believed that even by taking every precaution and using the latest technology the odds could only be slightly tipped in favour of a westward flight. 'The attempt by Captain Hinchliffe and the Honourable Elsie Mackay,' wrote one paper, 'was one of those which must be classed in the special category of sport and adventure. These two didn't seek to advertise any special kind of engine or even to beat any record. It is even doubtful if they seriously considered winning that $25,000 prize or sought especially the glory of being the first to cross the ocean in a single leap from east to west. Certainly they sought no publicity for themselves and their adventure before they took the risk. It was sport alone which led them on and has carried the Honourable Elsie Mackay to such a tragic destiny.' *Le Matin* added that it did not understand the 'peculiarities of the Anglo-Saxons' to undertake such an adventure not for glory or money but 'just because it was very exciting.'

Due to the experiences of previous aviators like Ruth Elder, who had been amazingly rescued from the sea when her plane came down near the Azores, and Harry Hawker, who seemed to be lost without trace in 1919 but who turned up a week later having been picked up by a ship without wireless, there remained some hope that a miracle would happen for Hinchliffe and Mackay. The remoteness of Labrador and the Newfoundland coast also continued to offer a faint lifeline that they may have survived a crash landing. Aviators and meteorologists familiar with the dangers of the Atlantic began to fear that the daring couple had not even reached half way before the sleet, ice and fog known to have extended that far across the ocean would have brought them down. Even if they'd reached Labrador an attempted landing at that time of year would have been as fatal as landing in mid-Atlantic. Experts quoted in *The New York Times* said: 'There were manyfold hazards also in the Atlantic which Captain Hinchliffe probably did not know of when he left Ireland (sic). The Atlantic in the eastern portion up to the mid ocean is at this time of year a place of fog and sleet because of the warm temperature caused by the Gulf Stream and the currents from the Azores. Sleet storms blow down from the north on the edge of this section and it is regarded as by far the most dangerous part of his journey. Many aviators do not believe that he even reached mid-Atlantic but that weighted down with ice which destroyed the lift of his wings he plunged into the water less than half way to his goal.' The writer concluded that 'between ice and storm the journey would have been one of tremendous peril.'

Airmen began to express their amazement that such an experienced aviator should have taken off at all in such treacherous winter conditions. When Captain Hinchliffe was waiting at Cranwell in the autumn of 1927 for an opportunity to 'hop' across the Atlantic with Charles Levine, he was asked by reporters why he did not make a start. He was reported as replying angrily: 'I am not going to commit suicide. I am not going out on a wild adventure. Do you believe for a moment that I would start out knowing it was an absolute certainty that I would come down in the Atlantic?'

In a profile of the captain published by *The New York Times* six months after the loss of the Endeavour, the aviation correspondent attempted to make sense of the famous flyer's actions. In the months after the disappearance of the aeroplane, there was speculation that it was news of the German plans to attempt the flight that had made him leave, or that Miss Mackay had put him under pressure to fly before her parents returned from Egypt. The mystery and secrecy surrounding the venture prompted some reporters to print rumours of a romance between the couple.

Friends of Hinch dismissed the theories and told *The Times* aviation correspondent that they knew he had favoured postponing the flight until April or May but a series of unfortunate incidents compelled him to make the flight when he had, or it would never have happened. They knew that he was a devoted family man and ordinarily opposed to women flying but Miss Mackay had been the only person in Britain prepared to finance the venture. They told journalists that the blame for the untimely departure lay entirely with the British Air Ministry: 'It was the Air Ministry which ordered him to remove the plane from Cranwell, said to be the only field in the British Isles from which Hinchliffe could take off with an adequate supply of fuel.'

After receiving the telegram from the Air Ministry on March 9th, Hinch had been unable to move the plane because of heavy snow falls. As he waited he obtained measurements from Baldonnel Field near Dublin but calculated that the lifting power of his plane would not allow him to take off from there with sufficient fuel for the flight. He also knew that even if Imperial Airways gave him permission to fly from Croydon it was doubtful that the length of the runway there was any greater than Baldonnel. The article, under the headline 'An Ill Fate Pursued Captain Hinchliffe', stated that: 'on the evening of March 12th the Atlantic weather report was better; in fact almost favourable. Miss Mackay had assured him that the insurance matter was attended to and had given him a receipt for a payment she had made to the insurance company. Hinchliffe, his back to the wall, weighed the risks. He knew it was a long chance but it was the only one he had.'

The New York Herald Tribune told its readers that 'the fate of Captain Hinchliffe and Miss Mackay is identical with that of other martyrs of aviation of whom it has never been possible to report anything more than "lost at sea".'

CHAPTER SEVEN

Sunshine Left His Heart

In the weeks and months following the loss of the *Endeavour*, the families of Hinchliffe and Mackay found themselves repeatedly in the headlines. The story of the flight moved in twists and turns that no one could have predicted. Being thrown into the spotlight in this way was intensely painful for the Inchcape family, who had to come to terms with the fact that not only had their precious but defiantly independent daughter secretly gone on the flight after all but, also, that she had lost her life somewhere in the hundreds of miles of unforgiving waves.

In complete despair Lord Inchcape and his wife, who was still in delicate health, left Cairo for London on March 25th. Emilie Hinchliffe, though equally grief stricken, at least had the advantage of having been involved with her husband's ambitions and plans. She had lived with an awareness of the risks he was taking for many months but the reality of the loss was nevertheless devastating, especially as she had two children to care for, the youngest, Pamela, was only four months old.

In a book written by Emilie some months later, she described the dawning realisation that the flight had failed: 'Departure on the great adventure from Cranwell! Authentic news of the machine's passage over the Irish Coast at 1.40pm the same day!! Then silence ... a silence rendered the more terrible by virtue of the previous supreme confidence in complete success. During the days and weeks that followed I kept on hoping against hope that some tidings might come from him; that perhaps he had been saved, or landed in a district where it was impossible to communicate. I prayed earnestly and fervently that my husband might be brought back to me.' Emilie wrote of briefly feeling a renewed hope when, exactly a month after the *Endeavour's* take-off, news was wired around the world that the German-Irish Atlantic attempt had crash-landed in Labrador, leading to speculation that the *Endeavour* might have suffered the same fate and there might finally be some concrete news of the British aviators.

The crew of the *Bremen* first made an attempt on the east to west crossing in August 1927 when they battled stormy weather for five hours after passing over Ireland before eventually being forced back to safety. Although not a new design, the Junkers W-33L was a remarkably advanced plane compared to other machines chosen for the Atlantic attempts. It was an all-metal construction, including its 'skin', which was made of corrugated Duralumin. It was the first low-wing plane to be flown over the Atlantic and had a span of just over 58 feet. Powered by a single six-cylinder Junkers engine, it had a top speed of 120 miles per hour, though the speed was probably restricted to nearer one hundred miles per hour due to the added weight of the fuel.

In April 1928 the original crew of Captain Koehl and Baron Von Hunefeld was joined by Irish aviator Commandant Fitzmaurice when the original co-pilot quit following an argument. Von Hunefeld had to act as interpreter as the two pilots didn't speak a word of each other's languages. They decided to take off from Baldonnel Field, though this was not without challenges over and above the usual. The aircraft wheels had initially sunk into the turf but when they finally got going and up to speed, a sheep wandered across the runway. Fitzmaurice barely got over it, causing the plane to bump up and down; Koehl thought it was the end and expected the plane to burst into flames.

Even in the air, the plane struggled to gain any kind of height; the undercarriage dragged through the tops of a small copse of trees and then the wing hit a hedge during a low turn. But it seems the luck of the Irish was with this flight. Like the *Endeavour*, the aircraft did not carry a wireless and, after leaving the Irish coast at County Galway at 7.20am on April 12th, nothing was heard of the plane. Everyone expected that this was yet another attempt that would be filed under the headline 'valiant losses'.

Despite a number of different problems, including a snapped fuel pipe, the lights failing on the instruments, headwinds that reduced their speed to only sixty miles per hour and the loss of their compass, which meant they had only a hazy idea of where they were, the crew of the *Bremen* eventually spotted a barren, frozen landscape and what appeared to be a ship caught in the ice but was, in fact, a lighthouse.

The end of the flight was described by Edward Jablonski in his 1972 book *Atlantic Fever*: 'They had no idea of their whereabouts but it was a definite port in a storm – and they had to alight somewhere soon. Circling the snow-incrusted rubble, Koehl spotted a small, reasonably smooth area, obviously a frozen-over pond. This would have to serve, so he set the plane down onto it as gently as possible. The wheels touched the surface, the plane settled down and suddenly there was a lurching crunch as the landing gear ripped away when it struck an outcropping of ice. The *Bremen* skidded, tipped onto the nose, damaging the propeller, and then ground to a stop in a flurry of snow. None of the men aboard the Junkers was injured and – wherever they were – they were safe after thirty-six and one half hours of gruelling, blind and confusing flying.'

They were on Greenly Island, with its population of fourteen, and they were a thousand miles off course. Eight years later the solo aviatrix Beryl Markham spoke of the narrow margin between the success and failure of her east to west flight. After her own emergency landing she told reporters: 'When I came down in the bog on Cape Breton Island there wasn't one drop [of petrol] left in the tanks. I'd been flying for only twenty-one hours and thought I had enough for twenty-eight. Fifteen seconds more and I believe my aeroplane and I would have gone down on the water and no one would have ever known what became of us.'

Sadly it appeared that the narrow margin between success and tragedy had not worked in favour of Hinchliffe and Mackay. Weeks passed and there was no news. The success of the *Bremen* was particularly difficult news to accept following the loss of the *Endeavour* for friends of Elsie who revealed the contents of some of her last letters. In October she had written of her desire to finance an Atlantic flight and go herself. "I want to do something that is going to benefit Britain and British aviation." In her letter she described her desire to land in Hyde Park in London at the end of their return flight so she could "arouse a greater national interest in aviation." Her final letter to her friend had been sent the day before the dramatic take-off, in it she wrote "Captain Hinchliffe has told me that we can leave in the morning and by the time you get this we shall be well away. I know we shall get there."

Instead it had become clear that the attempt had failed and the two aviators were lost without trace. On top of her bereavement, Emilie Hinchliffe faced a new difficulty: the wages due to her husband from Elsie Mackay, along with the insurance that had been arranged, were not forthcoming. The family solicitor discovered that Elsie's estate had been frozen and was in the hands of the trustee, her father. Emilie learned that two hours after the take-off from Cranwell a letter had arrived at the airfield addressed to Miss Mackay. It was from the insurance company stating that an additional sum would have to be paid before it would accept the risk on Captain Hinchliffe's life. The insurance Elsie believed she had arranged was invalid. This was a further blow to the grieving widow, left penniless with two very young daughters to support.

The newspapers discovered this new aspect to the fascinating Hinchliffe and Mackay story and ran with it, especially when reporters discovered that Emilie had written about the insurance issue to Lord Inchcape but he had not responded. Headlines depicted the wealthy peer as a cold, unfeeling man who had turned his back on a young mother left a widow and without a penny because of his daughter. In America, *Time* magazine described Lord Inchcape as 'that stern, rich shipping tycoon' who had been 'vexed and mortified' when his daughter set out to fly the Atlantic. The article stated that: 'Captain Hinchliffe's widow and child (sic) now reduced to penury have appealed in vain for assistance from stern Viscount Inchcape.'

Journalists seized on the news that Elsie had left an estate of £682,517 (Hinchliffe left only £22 14s 10d) – clearly more than enough to cover the promised insurance and outstanding wages. Various theories about the problems with the insurance were aired across the columns and there were suggestions that there had been a rift between Elsie and her father due to her escapades. However, there can be little doubt that the public silence and refusal to comment on the insurance matter were entirely due to grief and Lord Inchcape's 'very natural dislike to the tragic death of his daughter being a subject of public discussion', as it was described by a more sympathetic writer some time later.

With the insurance issue still rumbling on, a new and completely bizarre slant to the ongoing story appeared to add to the Inchcapes' torment. The newspapers were soon full of claims that posthumous messages were being related allegedly from Captain Hinchliffe to his widow through a spiritual medium. The news was broken by none other than the author of the Sherlock Holmes stories, Sir Arthur Conan Doyle, who was also well known for having a keen interest in spiritualism.

It seemed that a woman called Beatrice Earl, completely unconnected with the Hinchliffes, regularly tried to communicate with her son who had been killed in the First World War. Instead she had started to receive messages that appeared to make no sense to her and were clearly not from her son. The messages continued and, she claimed, were insistent; finally, from their content, she concluded that they related to the recent Atlantic aviation tragedy. Not knowing what to do with these messages, she wrote to Emilie Hinchliffe and sent details of what she had received to Sir Arthur, who had a regular newspaper column dealing with matters to do with his belief in spiritualism and the search to prove life after death. The letters were sent just as the Bremen made its flight to North America.

Sir Arthur was convinced that Mrs Earl was genuine but, before approaching Emilie Hinchliffe, he set up a series of séances with a leading medium in London. Eventually Emilie was informed of the messages and, although initially sceptical, Hinchliffe's widow became so convinced of their truth that she was converted to spiritualism, writing a book about her experiences and going on a sell-out lecture tour.

Emilie was quoted in *The Sunday Express* as saying that she had not been interested in spiritualism and that 'when the medium wrote to me saying she had a message from my husband I did not believe her. Later however, Sir

Arthur Conan Doyle wrote and asked me to accept the medium's message. I have met her a number of times since then and have received so many convincing messages of intimate detail from my husband that I am perfectly satisfied that this is his own version of the flight.'

She proceeded to explain that in one of the séances he had described what had happened, saying that: 'after passing over Mizzen Head, in the North of Ireland, we steered west-north-west for 850 miles. The weather was good, but cloudy and there was a little fog. This was between 2pm and 10pm, and our speed was eighty to ninety miles per hour. At 10pm we began to encounter bad weather, but our spirits were high, and we were still going well. We increased our speed to 100 miles an hour up to midnight, and went in a more northerly direction. We had gone, roughly speaking, 900 miles before we ran into bad weather. We ran right into the teeth of a terrific gale – wind, sleet and rain. The wind broke the left strut and ripped the fabric. I saw that further headway was impossible, and I deliberately altered my course to the south, hoping to fly out of the gale and reach the Azores. We flew south from midnight till 3am gradually coming down lower. At 1am, however, I knew that we were beaten as the compass had gone wrong and one of the plugs was missing. When Miss Mackay realised this she became unconscious and never recovered. I carried on the best way I could for two more hours and at 3am landed in the water one mile north of the Azores. We did not crash. I took a last drink of tea from my flask and set out to swim for the shore. I swam for twenty minutes but the currents were too strong and I became unconscious and was finally drowned. Miss Mackay's end was peaceful. She was drowned in the machine while still unconscious.'

The Inchcape family chose to keep a dignified silence on this subject but clearly the continued public interest in the story of Hinchliffe and Mackay caused considerable distress. In her book *The Return of Captain W. G. R. Hinchliffe*, Emilie was not allowed to mention the name of her husband's co-pilot, and during the tour she was legally prevented from discussing Elsie's involvement in the flight.

The story of the messages sent by Captain Hinchliffe and how they related to yet another aviation tragedy – the flight of the R101 airship – is told in great detail in the book *The Airmen Who Would Not Die* by John G. Fuller, which includes a curious incident reported some years later. According to Fuller, at about 2am on March 14th, about eighteen hours after the *Endeavour* took off, two RAF officers were asleep on board the P&O ship *Barabool* on their way back from a tour of duty in South Africa. They were old friends of Captain Hinchliffe but, as they had been at sea, they knew nothing of the Atlantic attempt. Squadron Leader Rivers Oldmeadow was asleep in his cabin when the door burst open. Reaching for his light he saw his friend Colonel G. L. P. Henderson standing in the doorway, clearly in a state of distress. He eventually explained that he had been woken by an apparition of Captain Hinchliffe, unmistakeable because of his distinctive eye patch, saying over and over, 'Hendy what am I going to do? I've got this woman with me and I'm lost. I'm lost.' Three days later a ship's news sheet was posted on the bulletin board – the headline reading that Captain Hinchliffe was missing after a transatlantic attempt. The two men only revealed their ghostly encounter many years later.

Lord Inchcape was left to deal with the very practical issue of his missing daughter's considerable estate. At the beginning of July it was announced that it was going to be generously presented to the British nation, the family declaring that they had no desire to profit in any way from Elsie's death. Winston Churchill, then Chancellor of the Exchequer, announced in Parliament that he had received and accepted 'an important gift to the nation in memory of the Hon Elsie Mackay who perished in attempting the passage of the Atlantic in an aeroplane. Their wish is that this gift should ultimately be applied in reduction of the National Debt. They propose that it should accumulate for a period of, roughly, fifty years, unless by some earlier date the proceeds, with other funds available, should be sufficient to redeem the whole of the liabilities of the State. This fund will accordingly be called The Elsie Mackay Fund.'

By 1976 the fund had reached a value of almost £5,000,000 and it was used as it was intended – to help towards the National Debt, which had by then reached £60,000,000. Such donations towards the National Debt were not unusual; Lord Inchcape's was the second half million presented in 1928. Gifts from as little as £43 to £100,000 had been presented during the previous ten years. *The Manchester Guardian* noted that there was a 'special poignancy' about Lord Inchcape's gift, made as a memorial to his daughter.

Aviator Jim Mollison later wrote in *The Book of Famous Flyers* that 'this was the sequel to the saddest chapter in the history of flyers. Thereafter designers wrestled with the problems set them by the Atlantic failures. As in all advances of science, however, the pioneers must risk their lives and die that those who come after may reap the benefit of their perilous adventuring.'

The newspaper reporters working for titles owned by Lords Beaverbrook and Rothermere were less sympathetic towards Lord Inchcape and continued to highlight the plight of Emilie Hinchliffe. Aviation was a small world and Captain Hinchliffe had been a famous, well-respected and well-connected pilot. Sir Sefton Brancker, Director of Civil Aviation and the British Air Ministry, had been a friend and he now used his position and influence to bring some kind of aid to his friend's widow. Eventually questions were raised in the House of Commons as Captain Hinchliffe had been in receipt of a wounds pension and disability retired pay for war service, but both of these small incomes had ceased with his death.

The flood of news articles on the matter brought no public reaction from Lord Inchcape despite actions like that of Lady Houston, the widow of a rival millionaire shipping tycoon, who sent £100 to Emilie as a token reminder to the head of P&O that others were concerned with the young mother's situation. The conditions of the gift of Elsie's estate to the British nation meant that Emilie would never be able to receive what, some argued, was her rightful share. Members of Parliament tried to secure some kind of Air Ministry award but it was made clear that these were not available to civilian flyers and Captain Hinchliffe had not remained in the RAF reserve. However, on the last day of July, Winston Churchill again made an announcement in the House of Commons, a statement that was totally unexpected. 'Lord Inchcape', he began, 'being desirous that the Elsie Mackay Fund of £500,000 sterling, given by him and Lady Inchcape and their family to the nation, should not be the occasion or object of any complaint by other sufferers from the disaster in which his daughter lost her life, has placed at the disposal of the Chancellor of the Exchequer a further sum of £10,000 sterling from his own property to be applied for the purpose of meeting any complaint in such manner as the Chancellor of the Exchequer in his absolute discretion may think fit. The Chancellor of the Exchequer has handed the sum of £10,000 sterling to the Public Trustee for administration accordingly.'

As Emilie Hinchliffe was the only person to fit into this category it was clear that Lord Inchcape had made a financial gesture equal to the insurance his daughter thought she'd arranged for her pilot. *The Manchester Guardian* reported that Mrs Hinchliffe was relieved and grateful for this recompense. She told reporters that it had come 'just in the nick of time. Since my husband's death I have been living on my small capital and I could not have gone on much longer. I should have been obliged to leave my house at Purley and really I do not know what would have happened.' She added that she was 'very grateful to Lord Inchcape, especially as he has apparently given this sum out of his own pocket'. The announcement had relieved her mind 'of a great deal of anxiety'.

Only days after this significant financial gesture the Hinchliffe and Mackay story reappeared in the headlines because a message was discovered in a bottle washed up on the shore in Wales. A man called George Dean of Flint discovered the bottle, which was tightly corked and contained a message written on a sheet torn from a pocket book. It was claimed that it said 'goodbye all, Elsie Mackay and Captain Hinchliffe. Down in fog and storm.' Although the bottle was handed in to the local police and it was immediately considered to be a hoax, such bottles had been found following other flights.

A discovery on a beach in County Donegal, Ireland, in December 1928 was given much more credence. In March 1929 Emilie Hinchliffe received a letter from the British Air Ministry informing her that part of an undercarriage had been found bearing serial numbers and a manufacturer's address: 76168547 Goodrich Silvertown Cord Airplane 150/508 Manufactured by the Goodrich

Company, Akron, Ohio, USA. Official enquiries brought the confirmation that the tyre belonged, without doubt, to the *Endeavour*. The discovery of the undercarriage was final proof that the plane and its crew had come down somewhere in the Atlantic and the two courageous aviators were lost forever.

The undercarriage discoverd on the Irish coast.
(photograph courtesy of Laurie Notaro)

For Emilie there was some interest in where the wreckage washed up as she believed it confirmed the truth of the psychic messages she believed she had received from her husband. Through these supernatural communications, Captain Hinchliffe had indicated that the plane had been forced down near the Azores, the collection of islands that had also featured in the flights of Ruth Elder and Lilli Dillenz. Emilie, with help from friends who were also aviation experts at the Ministry, had plotted the movement of the Gulf Stream. They had drawn the conclusion that any wreckage from the *Endeavour* would have been carried south past the Canaries and on to the West Indies or north, where the North Atlantic Drift would have taken it towards the west coast of Ireland – the exact spot where the undercarriage was discovered. Emilie was so convinced of this theory that she left instructions in her will that after her death her ashes should be scattered over the sea near to Corvu, the place in the Azores referred to by the medium. This was carried out in 1982 by her granddaughter who, like her mother, aunt and grandfather had become a pilot, fulfilling the wish that Emilie's remains could be somehow reunited with her husband.

Towards the end of 1928, the media circus had a new female aviator to focus their spotlight on. Amelia Earhart, as a passenger on the *Friendship* seaplane, became the first woman to cross the Atlantic, gaining the title Elsie Mackay and so many other brave women had yearned for. The west-to-east flight was in a three-engine Fokker monoplane and Miss Earhart had been invited along as a passenger by the sponsor, Mrs Frederick Guest, who believed that if a woman took part in the flight it would help change attitudes towards women's involvement in aviation. Although Miss Earhart will always be remembered for this achievement, on this occasion she played no active part in the flight and in fact described herself as being 'as useful as a sack of potatoes'. She was almost universally celebrated for the flight and dubbed 'Lady Lindy' but there was some criticism, one writer saying that her fame as an international heroine had been 'simply and solely because, owing to good luck and an airman's skill and efficiency, she is the first woman to travel from America to Europe by air.'

Four years later she answered such critics by flying solo across the Atlantic from America to Ireland – though she had been aiming for mainland Europe. In the same year British aviator Jim Mollison, who would later fly from east to west with his wife Amy Johnson, became the first solo flyer to complete the eastward route. It would be a further eight years before a woman flew the Atlantic in this direction solo. This honour went to the extraordinary Beryl Markham, who went despite her sponsor saying to her that he 'wouldn't tackle it for a million. Think of all that black water! Think how cold it is.'

Although Lord Inchcape was frequently described as a cold-hearted man and there were rumours of a rift with his daughter, it was clear from his actions during the months following the flight that he had been a loving and devoted father, left devastated by her loss. No doubt he had been furious at her secret plans but he was completely distraught at her death. His reluctance to speak to reporters displayed his distaste for the public discussion of his daughter's demise and his need to grieve privately with his wife and family.

The third Lord Inchcape spoke to journalists in 1977, when the Elsie Mackay Fund matured and was used to pay off some of the National Debt. He had vivid memories of his young aunt and was at Eton when he saw the evening newspaper headlines declaring her death. 'It was a terribly dramatic affair at the time. I remember the glamorous pictures of her in flying clothes. Had she lived she would have been another Amy Johnson. She was not a flighty type. She was very determined and serious about flying. But her death was a subject never spoken about as I grew up. She had defied his wishes. It was a terrible waste of a life. My grandfather was in the cast of the old ship owners, a very powerful personality.'

As that charismatic man grew older, he tired of the weight of responsibility of business affairs at his office in Leadenhall Street in London and turned more and more to the comfort and solace of his family. He found fresh joy in the lives of his grandchildren but his enduring sorrow was the loss of his determined daughter. Official biographer Hector Bolitho wrote that the uncertainty and horror of her death haunted Lord Inchcape for the rest of his life. One of Elsie's sisters told Bolitho that a year after the tragedy she had been dining alone with her father in silence when he looked up dismally from his meal and said: 'I wonder how she did die.'

During what was to be the last chapter of her life Elsie had become very close to her father, working for P&O and living either at the family home in London or at Carlock House on the Glenapp estate. One of her sisters later said: 'There is no doubt that after Elsie's death some of the sunshine went out of my father's heart. I do not think that life was ever the same for him.'

The depth of his mourning is clear from the memorials he created for his courageous and independent daughter. In September 1929, the newly appointed Earl and Countess of Inchcape announced that they would be creating a stained-glass window in the parish church at Glenapp in memory of their daughter, the Honourable Elsie Mackay. At a ceremony in August the following year, the window was unveiled in the tiny church where Elsie had worshipped so often. The Earl and Countess had arranged for the chancel arch to be raised six feet to allow the installation of the window depicting the Lord risen and crowned in glory; the right panel featured a likeness of Elsie with her hand upraised, pointing to the crown. New windows of cathedral glass were added together with oak flooring, seating and panelling. An entrance porch was built and the Countess also gifted wall lamps carved in oak with Celtic symbols and an embroidered pulpit fall that had been created at the Royal Art School of Needlework in South Kensington.

Glenapp Church near Ballantrae.
(photograph author's own)

During the dedication service Dr John White, then the Moderator of the General Assembly of the Church of Scotland, unveiled the memorial 'to the glory of God and in memory of a loving and much loved daughter, Elsie Mackay, who lost her life in an exploit of daring adventure which thrilled the heart of the community, inspiring others to face risks heroically in the cause of progress and for the glory of human achievement.' Referring to the miracles of science, telegraphy, wireless and aerial travel, he added: 'Twenty-seven years ago Orville Wright astonished the world by flying 950 feet. Today the nations are linked by aircraft. This achievement has been the result, not only of scientific progress but of the bold and venturesome spirit of men and women. There could be no progress without sacrifice and heavy toll had been paid; but it was manifest that we were not living in days that had suffered any eclipse in courage and endurance.'

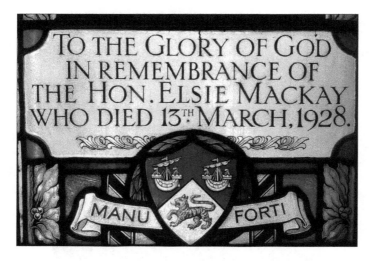

Detail from the stained glass window in Glenapp Church.
(photograph author's own)

Perhaps more poignantly, the Earl and Countess arranged for rhododendron and azalea bushes to be planted on the hillside opposite the tiny kirk. The bushes spelt out her name, Elsie, in letters more than fifty feet across, as if her father was trying somehow to call her spirit home. Although they are largely overgrown now, it is possible still to make out the original shapes. The intense feeling of loss experienced by so many in Glenapp and Ballantrae at the death of this charming, bright and caring young woman was writ large for all to see.

Despite his great wealth and power, it was to this small church in a remote

Scottish glen that the body of the Earl of Inchcape was returned following his death from heart failure. He spent most of the last few years of his life either on his yacht *The Rover* or at Glenapp Castle, although he never fully retired from his business interests. He died in his eightieth year aboard *The Rover* when it was anchored near Monte Carlo, just four years after Elsie's disappearance. His remains were returned to Glenapp for burial in an impressive tomb that lies behind the church. The Countess had two windows installed in his honour above the entrance designed by Douglas Strachan.

The overgrown hillside as seen from Glenapp Church.
(*photograph author's own*)

Glenapp Castle and the little church were places of great importance to the Inchcapes. In return, the Mackay family were held in high regard and remembered with great warmth and affection. In an article about Glenapp published in *The Gallovidian* magazine in 1930 a local man was quoted referring to Carlock House, an estate property that Elsie often used, saying: 'Oh dear me, but it's a lanely, lanely hoose since Miss Elsie passed awa'. I often think that as she looked doon that bonnie glen an' saw Finnart Bay glintin in the sunshine, that it fired her imagination to flee ower the Atlantic. Man, if she had only succeeded she wad ha'e been hailed as the bravest wumman the worl' had ever seen – an' cud she be ony less brave because she failed?

There's nae a hoose in Glenapp an' for miles aroun' whaur her memory isna held dear – an her love o' the place an' her kindness to everybody aboot it had earned her that place in oor hearts. The Hon Miss Elsie sowed whaur Miss Amy Johnstone (sic) reaped, and baith ha'e done much to put woman on an equality wi' man.'

Detail from the stained glass window in Glenapp Church.
(photograph author's own)

✦

A small report that was not picked up by the British press appeared in *The New York Times* in August 1928. It stated that plane wreckage had been sighted north-east of Newfoundland. More than seventy years later the article was discovered in the archives by aviation historian Quentin Wilson. The report said that information was received from St John's, Newfoundland, on August 13th: 'The steamship *Seapool* wirelessed here at 8am Eastern Standard Time, that it had sighted an airplane or seaplane but had failed to salvage it owing to the darkness. Five feet of the rudder of the plane were showing above water, and part of the damaged body and wing was awash, the message added. The color was undistinguishable and the shape of the machine showed that it had been a long time in the water. The ship's position is about 400 miles north east from here. Local mariners think the wreck may be that of the Hinchliffe plane.' Further news of this incident, like the wreckage itself, then sank without trace but it leaves a tantalising clue that perhaps, after all, Elsie and Hinch almost made it.

Postscript

Ten years after the tragic events of Elsie's Atlantic attempt, her name returned to the headlines in a curious story that claimed she was still alive. The source was her former husband, actor Dennis Wyndham. The 'fantastic theory' was that the errant heiress had been secretly living in South America since the flight. There was widespread coverage around the British Empire of the claim by Dennis that he did not believe that the plane in which she'd flown had crashed in mid-Atlantic, leading to her death. His bizarre story put forward the theory that Elsie had safely crossed the Atlantic, landing in some 'lonely part of the American continent.' He told journalists, 'I have never for one moment held the belief that Elsie is dead and recently I received a piece of evidence that has strengthened that belief.'

Dennis claimed that before she left, Elsie told him she had bought a boy's wig and intended stepping from the plane disguised as a male mechanic. The new evidence he had discovered was the story of a ship's officer who once worked for P&O and knew Elsie personally from her period with the company. 'This officer,' Dennis said, 'had just returned from Lima in Peru. There he heard of a mysterious Englishwoman who was living a hermit life in a little house on the outskirts. She had been there for more than nine years. No one had ever learned her name or anything about her.' The officer wondered if he could do anything to aid this fellow countrywoman but, when he called at the house, she bluntly refused to see him 'but he caught a glimpse of a white face through a window. He told me he recognised the features at once, wan and weary though they were.'

Dennis claimed that he had been deeply stirred by the story as he had always known Elsie was not dead. 'I have been present at many séances at which what purported to be her voice came through from the other side. On every occasion I was sceptical. The reason was simple. There was a nickname she had always used when referring to me. No one could have invented a name like it. Once we arranged that if ever either of us after death wished to get into communication from the spirit world that nickname should be given. At séances I have time and again asked for the voice to give this code. Never has it been given.'

Of course this story says more about the continued interest in Elsie Mackay ten years after she'd gone missing, and possibly more about the state of Dennis Wyndham's career, than it sheds any real light on what happened to the flight. The idea that they could have landed anywhere without being seen is absolutely absurd, given the remote locations where possible sightings were reported in the hours after the take off. There is no explanation as to why Elsie would wish to escape parents she was clearly devoted to, and there is no mention of Captain Hinchliffe in this bizarre tale. However, rumours of a romance between the two inevitably cropped up in the years following their disappearance including one, sometimes discussed in the small village of Ballantrae where Elsie had been such a feature of local life, that the pair had flown off to the Caribbean to start a new life together.

Although Elsie's name was largely forgotten elsewhere in the world, her memory lived on amongst the community of the small south Ayrshire village. One resident said that her mother, who had lived on the estate, always spoke fondly of 'Miss Elsie' and often sighed, 'I wonder what happened to Elsie.' When Glenapp Castle was restored in the late twentieth century, the new owners closed the gates at the front of the mansion only to be told in no uncertain terms by a local resident that this was a terrible thing to do: 'The gates should never be closed until Elsie comes back.' Given this was more than seventy years after the flight, this was, of course, highly unlikely. The charming story also proved to be misleading as it was later discovered that the gates had only been erected in the 1960s.

My motivation for writing this book was an attempt to put the record straight. Elsie Mackay's failure to achieve her goal of being the first woman to fly the Atlantic led her to become a footnote in aviation history. Too often her name was only mentioned as part of the supernatural story that followed

Captain Hinchliffe after the flight. Too often she was dismissed from any serious consideration as an aviator; when I first heard about her, she was being treated in this way, and hers was an offbeat tale of an heiress with more money than sense. But I was captivated and felt that this courageous young woman had been done a disservice.

In 1936 a series of articles was published in *The Sunday Graphic and Sunday News* as a celebration of the early pioneer pilots who were prepared to risk their lives to conquer the Atlantic. That year the first Transatlantic Air Service was expected to open between Europe and America. The very first article in the series, written by Clifford W. Collinson and Captain F. McDermott, was about Elsie Mackay. They recognised that her 'brave effort' had become obscured, partly because of her father's dislike of his daughter's tragic death being the subject of public discussion. Although the authors stated that they understood the family's natural desire not to have their grief exploited, they argued that the British nation 'should pay tribute to those of its daughters, just as much as its sons, who lose their lives in an endeavour to bring honour to the mother country.' They felt that her attempt had been unjustly accused of being foolhardy and embarked on without adequate preparation. In their opinion this was contrary to the facts, as they hoped to prove with their article.

Elsie was not attempting the flight as a passenger or just the sponsor. Both Captain and Emilie Hinchliffe spoke of Elsie's involvement in the arduous test flights and knew that she would have played a crucial role in the flight itself. Aviation historian Quentin Wilson believes that, due to the positioning of the cockpit, Elsie would have played a key role in trimming the aircraft.

It was also her good judgement and intelligence that brought her to approach Captain Hinchliffe in the first place. There was general agreement in the aviation community at the time that no other flier had dedicated more time and effort into planning the flight.

In this modern age of flight, it is hard to understand the physical fitness and mental resolve, together with confidence and courage, that were necessary for these early aviators to even contemplate record-breaking flights. We can only imagine how Hinch and Elsie felt in that tiny cockpit, in the dark with only a faint glow from the instruments, battling the elements with limited visibility for hour upon hour, and their despair when all hope was lost and the plane was finally dragged down to the sea by the weight of ice that had formed on the fuselage.

We will probably never know how close they came to achieving their aim, though Quentin Wilson spent many years researching the flight and piecing together information on weather conditions, currents and possible sightings. *The New York Times* article about the wreckage spotted 400 miles from the Newfoundland coast in August 1928 poses the most tantalising clue. Wilson believed it was unlikely that the plane could have been the *Endeavour*, afloat five months after the flight, but if it was, where had it been until then? The plane was designed so that its empty petrol tanks would act as buoyancy if it was forced down in water, or perhaps they had crash landed on the icy wastes of Labrador and were either killed in the crash or died when rescue never came. As temperatures rose in the summer, the plane could have then found itself in water and been washed around the currents in the north Atlantic. This is obviously fanciful speculation but I, personally, like to believe that Hinchliffe and Elsie did somehow make it and she was the first woman to fly the Atlantic.

What is real is that the Honourable Elsie Mackay was an example of a thoroughly modern woman who helped to push forward the role of women in early-twentieth-century society. For a woman of her background and wealth it would have been easy to enjoy a life of ease, of useful charity work and marriage. At a time when many of her contemporaries were members of the 'bright young things', indulging in the high life of unconventional parties, drug taking and silly escapades, she chose instead to follow her father's example of hard work and dedication. In the worlds of acting, design and aviation she excelled and led the way for other women.

The Honourable Elsie Mackay was an extraordinarily talented, brave and, by all accounts, warm-hearted, generous and delightful person who deserves to be remembered.

APPENDIX

The Flight

By Quentin Wilson

Artistic impression of Elsie and Hinch sketched for an Australian
magazine article - the plane is clearly not a Stinson Detroiter.
(artist unknown)

The conventional wisdom is that an attempt to fly the North Atlantic
from east to west involves flying in a headwind – the prevailing westerly
so well known to those who live on the Atlantic coasts of Britain and Ireland.
But this was not what lay ahead of the *Endeavour* when it left Cranwell on
the morning of the 13th March. A large area of low pressure in mid-Atlantic
combined with high pressure over Iceland created a flow of air from east to
west over much of the region in which the aircraft as about to fly. This was
very significant for an aeroplane that normally cruised at an air speed of only
about 90 miles per hour. A head wind or tail wind of as little as ten miles per
hour would have a major influence on the speed of the aircraft over the sea,
and the wind speeds over the Atlantic were generally much greater than ten

miles per hour.

The information that led to these conclusions came in a large envelope delivered in response to a letter sent to the British Met. Office, at that time based in Bracknell. It seemed like a shot in the dark. "Do you have any information on the weather over the North Atlantic for 13th and 14th March 1928?" Included in the contents of the large envelope were two synoptic charts issued just after 1100 hours on the required dates, each covering a large area of the northern hemisphere. The charts showed the patterns of isobars and the 'contour' lines of equal pressure, which we now see so frequently on our television screens. What they did not show were the now familiar weather fronts. The reason for this was that the ideas and theory of weather fronts were relatively new. Developed by the Norwegian Professor Bjerknes they were not yet fully accepted by the British Met. Office and consequently were not shown on British synoptic charts. Again referring to what we see on our television screens, we are well aware that these weather fronts are usually associated with what we regard as bad weather, at times very bad weather.

So what did Hinchliffe know about the weather conditions about to be encountered over the Atlantic? The short answer is not very much. He would have had a verbal description of what was to be expected, much like a shipping forecast, from what was known of the pressure systems and from the shipping reports. But he would not have had any concept of the weather front swinging northwards about the Low in the North Atlantic. His first experience of that would have been the snow falling along the south coast of Ireland. RAF Cranwell was one of a number of stations around the UK where 'Upper Air Data' measurements were taken at various times each day. At 6.00 am at Cranwell on Tuesday 13th March the sky was cloudy and the air over the airfield was almost still. There was snow on the ground. But at a height of 1000 feet above the airfield there was a wind of about 20 miles per hour from the north-east. As the morning progressed the wind speeds at an altitude of about 1000 feet across the Midlands of England settled to between 11 and 14 miles per hour, sometimes assisting a westbound aeroplane, sometimes reducing its speed over the ground. The skies were generally cloudy.

The reports giving the time of departure of the *Endeavour* from Cranwell are not in precise agreement. *The Glasgow Herald* of the 14th March and the RAF *Cadet College Magazine* published in August 1928 gave the take-off time as 0845 hours, "after a run of nearly a mile across the snow" under a cloudy sky and with the temperature close to freezing; *The New York Times* stated 0835 and the London Times 0830 hours. The first reported sighting after leaving Cranwell was at about 1130 hours at Kilmeaden in County Waterford, a few miles inland from the south coast of Ireland. According to *The London Times* of 14th March, Civil Guards had reported having seen an aeroplane flying very fast and at a high altitude. Heavy snow was falling and visibility was low. It seems unlikely that the Detroiter would have been at high altitude under these conditions, and when it was still at high weight; but then, such observations are subjective. The next report was supplied from Dublin: "Commandant Fitzmaurice, Free State Air Force, Baldonnell, states that the man in charge of the lighthouse at Mizen Head, Co. Cork, reports an aeroplane passing over Mizen Head at 1.30pm. The officer in charge of the life-saving service at Crookhaven in the same area confirms the report."

The combination of the high take-off weight of the Detroiter, the Welsh mountains that lay like a barrier in the direct route from Cranwell to the south of Ireland, and the cloud cover, suggest strongly that on leaving Cranwell Hinchliffe would not have taken the direct route to the south of Ireland but would have followed a course to the south of the Peak District towards the Wirral, and would then have skirted the north coast of Wales to Anglesey before turning towards the south of Ireland. The straight line distance from Cranwell to Kilmeaden and then to Mizen Head is close to 400 statute miles. The route round the North Wales coast only increases this distance to 425 miles.

Using the known distances and times suggests that the time of the sighting at Kilmeaden is not accurate but the time given by the man in charge (of the signal station) at Mizen Head would have been accurate and almost certainly logged. The flight time from Cranwell to Mizen Head was between four hours 55 minutes and four hours 45 minutes, giving average speeds over 425 miles of 86 or 90 miles per hour. Allowing for a small average tail-wind component over the 425 miles indicates that the *Endeavour* was flying at an air speed of about 85 miles per hour in the early stages of the flight.

It was also reported from Mizen Head that the aeroplane was "flying due west on the ordinary steamship route". In order to travel by the shortest distance between two points on the earth's surface the track to be followed is known as a Great Circle course. If the Great Circle course from Mizen Head to, say St John's Newfoundland is drawn on a chart, or more easily on a globe of the world it becomes apparent that at Mizen Head the Great Circle course is almost exactly due west and would be the steamship route from the south of Ireland to ports on the eastern seaboard of America. The last sighting of the Detroiter as it headed out over the North Atlantic was from a steamship 170 miles from Ireland, giving a degree of confirmation that Captain Hincliffe was holding to the Great Circle route. Another feature of this route is the need for accurate navigation. Unlike a flight from St John's to Europe, which has a large land 'target' where a welcoming landfall can be made, errors on the east-west route can be severely punished. The navigational equipment on the Detroiter was very basic by today's standards and it was probable that the aircraft would deviate from the Great Circle course, either to the south or the north. An error to the south could mean that the crew of the *Endeavour* would not see Newfoundland and might then travel parallel to the east coast of Canada and the US for a very long way without ever sighting land. An error to the north could take the plane over Labrador and, while this would at least be a landfall, Labrador in March is a wilderness of ice and snow with very few habitations. Today, high flying jet airliners en route from the UK pass over this area and if passengers with a window seat are lucky and the air is clear, they can look down on this frozen wasteland and ponder what this might have meant for Captain Hinchliffe and Elsie Mackay. In fact there is not need to speculate for only a month after the flight of the *Endeavour* the German aircraft, *Bremen*, on an attempted east-west Atlantic crossing, made a forced landing near a manned lighthouse on a small island in the Belle Isle Strait after being lost and with the crew looking in vain for signs of life on the ground below.

Weather reports in the press of the weather conditions faced by Hinchliffe and Elsie in the North Atlantic tell different stories. A report in *The New York Times* of Tuesday 20th March said the United States liner *Republic* had berthed on the previous day at Hoboken from Bremen, Southampton, Cobh and Boston, 24 hours late due to the extreme weather in the North Atlantic. The captain said "the wind was so strong that the vessel had to heave to" ..... "strong westerly winds prevailed from the 13th to the 16th." The Met. Office synoptic charts of the time give few clues about the weather, with only isolated wind arrows showing estimates of wind speeds. A later analysis by the US Navy resulted in much more detailed information and much of what follows is based on these historical weather maps. The chart for 1300 hours GMT on 13th March 1928 shows the pressure system surrounding the mid-atlantic low of 990 millibar, as on the Met. Office chart, just to the south of the Great Circle route from Mizen Head. This pressure corresponds to 742mm or 29.2 inches of mercury on a standard household barometer, which is not a notably low pressure, corresponding only to the left hand edge of the word 'change' with which we are so well acquainted. A pressure corresponding to 'stormy' would be around 960 millibar and a very deep depression would be about 930 millibar. So what was driving the very bad conditions experienced by the liner *Republic*? The historical maps show high pressure gradients to the south of the Low and correspondingly high westerly wind speeds reaching Beaufort wind force 9, which is a strong gale with speeds in the range of 47 to 54 miles per hour. This is consistent with the report from the liner *Republic*. On the north side of the Low and along the Great Circle track wind conditions are much more favourable.

Calculation of wind speed and direction for every five degrees of longitude along the track from Mizen Head shows that at the start of the crossing the wind speed would have been about 24 mph from the south-east. This would have given a useful tail wind component to the *Endeavour* and would also have blown the aircraft towards the north if the pilots had not made allowance for drift. Since the available information is that the Endeavour was holding to the Great Circle route it must be assumed that the pilots were making this correction. On this basis, the time to reach each five degrees of longitude along the Great Circle can be calculated, with the results shown below in Greenwich Mean Time and as True Local Time which lags GMT by a third of an hour for each five degrees of longitude when travelling west.

Longitude Degrees West	GMT Decimal Hours	Local Time Decimal Hours	Time from Cranwell Decimal Hours (0845 start assumed)
10	13.50	12.83	4.75
15	15.71	14.71	6.96
20	17.88	16.55	9.13
25	19.98	18.31	11.23
30	21.96	19.96	13.21

Sunset at London on 11th March was at 5.57pm, let us say at 1800 hours GMT. Darkness depends on cloud cover and would be, at most, one hour after sunset or about 1900 hours local time. The table shows that from about 25 degrees west, when the *Endeavour* could have been in the air for about eleven hours, except for the faint glow of the instruments in the cockpit, Hinchliffe and Elsie would have been in darkness.

Carrying on further with this analysis shows that the *Endeavour* would have entered air streams that became progressively more northerly, reducing the true speed of the aircraft over the sea, but still resulting in a landfall in Newfoundland around 7.00 am local time. Is there any basis for believing that this might have happened? It was commented in the press at the time that when there was an Atlantic attempt there were always many reports of people hearing aircraft, most or all of which proved false. In the case of the Hinchliffe and Mackay flight there were similar reports from along the north-east seaboard. Most were soon discounted but two could have been correct: *The New York Times* of the 15th March quoted reports from Brigus in Newfoundland and Killigrews on Conception Bay, about 20 miles from St John's. Both reports placed the plane there early in the morning, which would be consistent with a landfall at around 7.00 am local time. Most other reports were much later in the day and one press item estimated that the plane might be due about noon. The possibility of the *Endeavour* making a fast time over the Atlantic is due to the easterly air circulation to the north of the Atlantic Low. Another factor is that the US Navy's Historical Weather Maps show that if the *Endeavour* had survived the weather front near Ireland it would not have encountered another frontal system before reaching Newfoundland, where the weather conditions, according to a 13th March Special Cable from St John's published in the 14th March edition of *The New York Times*, were stated to be "favourable for the landing of Captain Hinchliffe's plane if he succeeds in passing the ice floe region off the coast. It is improbable that he would be able to leave again, however, even if he lands anywhere in this country due to the deep snow. Harbor Grace airport is thickly covered with snow and every other level spot near by is also obstructed by a dense white covering".

It would be good to think that the *Endeavour* had succeeded in crossing the Atlantic but there are only little hints as to the probable end to the flight. What is known for certain is that the aircraft came down in the sea. A letter dated 1st March 1929 from the UK Air Ministry to Mrs Hinchliffe stated that the part of an aeroplane undercarriage washed ashore in County Donegal had been identified as coming from the *Endeavour*. This would be consistent with a sea landing when impact with the water or ice floes sheared off the aircraft undercarriage. More tantalising is the following report quoted verbatim from *The New York Times* of August 14th 1928 headlined "Sights Plane Wreck Afloat on Atlantic – Ship Radios Salvage Attempt Failed – Machine believed to have been Hinchliffe's.

St John's Newfoundland, Aug. 13 – The Steamship *Seapool* wirelessed here at 8 am, Eastern Standard Time, from latitude 51.36 N. and longitude 14.41 (sic) W. that it had sighted an airplane or seaplane but had failed to salvage it owing to the darkness. Five feet of the rudder of the plane were showing above the water, and part of the damaged body and wing was awash the message added. The color was undistinguishable and the shape of the machine showed that it had been a long time in the water. The ship's position is about 400 miles north-east from here. Local mariners think the wreck may be that of the Hinchliffe plane".

The latitude in this report was incorrectly stated. In correspondence with St John's journalist Gary Hebbard, the author of this Appendix was informed that the longitude in *The New York Times* report was a misprint. It should have read 44.41 W. When this is corrected, the reported position plots at 400 miles from St John's. Gary added the comment that the "wreckage, even from airplanes, has been known to float so long on occasion that it had to be deliberately sunk as a hazard to navigation". This leaves unanswered, possibly for ever, the question of where the wreck could have been for five months. The behaviour of ocean currents is very complex!

In attempting to disentangle at least some of the story of the flight of the *Endeavour* the author of this Appendix also wishes to acknowledge the considerable assistance of Meteorologists Bill Pike and Deborah Miles.

The Stinson Detroiter

The origins of the Detroiter are told in John W Underwood's book The Stinsons. Built initially as a biplane the Stinson SB-1 Detroiter was an innovative design that had an enclosed cockpit, cabin heating, wheel brakes and an electric starter. Successful though the SB-1 was Eddie Stinson recognised as early as 1926 that biplanes were obsolete. The Detroiter was redesigned as a monoplane and designated the SM-1 Detroiter unusually retaining the name of the earlier machine. It was entered in the 1927 Ford Tour, a two week event in which the SM-1 Detroiter triumphed easily over its rivals. In August 1927 pilots Brock and Schlee left Ford Airport in their monoplane Detroiter named *Pride of Detroit* on the first stage of their attempt to fly round the world. Using Harbour Grace in Newfoundland as the departure point for the Atlantic crossing the *Pride of Detroit* landed safely in England and then went on to cross Europe and Asia before the record attempt was abandoned due to unacceptable risks of the Pacific crossing, after completing two thirds of their planned round the world flight. It has been said that the Detroiter monoplanes were kept very busy making history and that just about every one built was off on some sort of record flight. These record-breaking attempts did involve risks and many aircraft, including Detroiters, and their crews were lost during this period. Nevertheless the SM-1 was clearly a very capable machine that would bring home its crew given a little luck and tolerable weather, so it was not surprising that this was the machine selected by Captain Hinchliffe for the Atlantic attempt. On March 28th 1928, two weeks after the disappearance of the *Endeavour* Eddie Stinson and George Haldeman, who had flown with Ruth Elder the previous year, took off in a Detroiter from an airfield in Florida landing two days later as joint holders of the world's endurance record after more than fifty three hours in the air, proving the capability of the aircraft.

Technical Details

(From US Civil Aircraft by Joseph P Juptner)

The Stinson Detroiter was a high wing monoplane with enclosed cockpit, dual controls and cabin seating for six passengers powered by a 220 HP Wright J-5C radial engine (the same engine used by Charles Lindberg on the *Spirit of St Louis*). It featured a horizontal stabiliser – tail plane – adjustable in flight. It had cabin heating, wheel brakes and an electric starter. The duel cockpit featured the tail plane trim lever on the left hand side. Due to Hinchliffe's damaged eye he always sat on the right hand side which meant that Elsie Mackay would have been responsible for the maintenance of the trim of the aircraft in pitch during the flight.

The plane had a wing span of 45 feet 10 inches, wing chord 84 inches, wing area 292 square feet and a fuselage width of about four feet 11/2 inches. It was 32 feet long and eight feet three inches high. With a maximum load of 3800 lbs it had a top cruising speed of 122 miles per hour. The basic price from the factory in 1928 was $12,500.

Weight Estimate for the *Endeavour* on Departure from Cranwell

According to the Autumn 1928 issue of the RAF *Cadet College Magazine* the fuel load of the *Endeavour* was made up of 180 gallons contained in wing tanks, 225 gallons in a large tank fitted in the cabin behind the two front seats, and 75 gallons in 17 specially made aluminium cans stacked behind the cabin tank. Each of these cans weighed ¾ lb empty. At 7.2 lb per imperial gallon the 480 gallons of fuel would weight 3456lb. Making guesses about the weights of Hinchliffe, Elsie Mackay and extra items added to the aircraft gives the following aircraft weight on departure from Cranwell on 13th March 1928.

SM-1 Detroiter empty weight	1970lb
480 gallons of fuel	3456lb
17 fuel cans	13lb

Hinchliffe at 180lb including clothing and food	180lb
Mackay at 140lb including clothing and food	140lb
Extra fuel tankage, piping, instruments etc	50lb

This gives an approximate take-off weight at Cranwell of 5809lb which is well above the manufacturers maximum weight of 3800lb. On take-off at Cranwell the *Endeavour* was loaded to over 50 per cent above the maximum design weight for the aircraft. This would have reduced the ability of the plane to accelerate resulting in much longer than normal take-off run and a slower rate of climb once off the ground. It would also have reduced the cruising speed and the height to which the aircraft could climb. Apart from these performance issues, overloading the aircraft by over 50 per cent was potentially very dangerous since the safety margins on the structure would have been of a similar order, risking structural failure of the fully fuelled *Endeavour* at the very beginning of the attempt on the Atlantic crossing.

Bibliography

Allen, Roy: *A Pictorial History of KLM Royal Dutch Airlines* (Ian Allan) 1978

Barker, Ralph: *Great Mysteries of the Air* (Javelin Books) 1966,

Beaty, David: *The Proving Flight* (Penguin) 1956

Bolitho, Hector: *James Lyle Mackay First Earl of Inchcape* (John Murray, London) 1936

Butler, Susan: *East to the Dawn: The Life of Amelia Earhart* (Da Capo Press) 1999

Cluett, Douglas: *The First, the Fastest and the Famous* (Sutton Libraries and Arts Services) 1985

Collinson, Clifford and McDermott, Captain F.: *Through Atlantic Clouds: The History of Atlantic Flight* (Hutchinson) 1934

Daily Express: *Those Tremendous Years 1919–1938* (London) 1938

Dixon, Charles: *The Conquest of the Atlantic by Air* (J. B. Lippincott Company) 1931

Franks, Norman and Dempsey, Harry: *Sopwith Camel Aces of World War 1* (Osprey Publishing) 2003

Fuller, John G.: *The Airmen Who Would Not Die* (Corgi) 1981

Gallovidian Annual (Robert Dinwiddie, Dumfries) 1930

Green, Peter and Hodgson, Mike: *Cranwell* (Midland Publishing) 1993

Hinchliffe, Emilie: *The Return of Captain W. G. R. Hinchliffe* (Psychic Press) 1930

Jablonski, Edward: *Atlantic Fever* (The Macmillan Company) 1972

Jones, Stephanie (*Trade and Shipping: Lord Inchcape 1852–1932*) Manchester University Press 1989

Learmonth, Bob, Nash, Joanna and Cluett, Douglas: *The First Croydon*

Airport 1915–1928 (Sutton Libraries and Arts Services) 1977

Lomax, Judy: *Women of the Air* (John Murray Ltd) 1986

Lovell, Mary S: *Straight on Till Morning* (St Martin's Press) 1987

McEwen, Yvonne: *It's a Long Way to Tipperary: British and Irish Nurses in the Great War* (Cualann Press) 2006

Markham, Beryl: *West With the Night* (North Point Press) 1983

Mollison, J. A.: *The Book of Famous Flyers* (Collins Clear Type Press) 1934

Partridge, Michael J: *Maverick Airman* (Eastbourne College Arnold Embellishers) 2010

Sayers, Dorothy L.: *Clouds of Witness* (Victor Gollancz Ltd) 1926

Sayers, Dorothy L.: *Unnatural Death* (Victor Gollancz Ltd) 1927

Spriggs, C. St John: *Great Flights* (Tomas Nelson and Sons) 1935

Taylor, D. J.: *Bright Young People: The Rise and Fall of a Generation 1918–1940* (Chatto and Windus) 2007

Underwood, John W: *The Stinsons* (Heritage Press) 1976

Van de Lemme, Arie: *A Guide to Art Deco Style* (Quintet Publishing) 1986

Wealleans, Anne: *Designing Liners: A History of Interior Design Afloat* (Routledge) 2006

Winchester, Simon: *Atlantic* (Harper Press) 2010

Newspapers

The Adelaide Chronicle

The Adelaide News

The Aero Digest

The Angus Evening Telegraph

The Australasian

Ayrshire Post

Carrick Herald

The Catholic Press
Daily Express
Daily Mirror
The Derby Daily Telegraph
The Dundee Courier and Advertiser
Girvan Town Crier and Pavilion News
The Glasgow Herald
Le Matin
Manchester Guardian
The New South Wales Leader
The New York Evening Sun
The New York Herald Tribune
The New York Times
The Richmond River Herald
Stranraer Free Press
Sunday Graphic and Sunday News
The Sydney Sun
The Times

Websites

The Cross and the Cockade International eGroup Archives

www.maaa.org

www.peerage.com

www.screenonline.org.uk

www.missinglinkclassichorror.co.uk

www.imdb.com

www.afleetingpeace.co.uk

www.wikipedia.com

Resources

The National Archives of Scotland, Edinburgh.

The British Library Newspaper Collection, Colindale.

The Australian Newspaper Library, Trove.

The Mitchell Library, Glasgow.

Private collection and correspondence with William Barraclough

Correspondence with Quentin Wilson

Correspondence with Laurie Notaro.

Acknowledgements

I am greatly indebted to Quentin Wilson who investigated the flight of Hinchliffe and Mackay for many years and who very generously shared his research with me; and also William Barraclough for generously sharing letters and photographs from his family archive. I would also like to thank Ballantrae librarian Janette McCulloch, David Barnes of the Cross and Cockade Society, author Dennis Sawden, the National Portrait Gallery for the permission to use the photograph of Dennis Wyndham (copyright William Hustler and Georgina Hustler), Random House for permission to use the photograph of the *Endeavour*, Golden Wings Flying Museum Minneapolis, USA for the images of the Stinson Detroiter and cockpit, and Mr and Mrs Cowan formerly of Glenapp Castle. Thanks also go to Reverend Jim Guthrie for permission to photograph the Glenapp Church Window and to the Royal Aero Club Trust for their permission to use the images of Captain Hinchliffe and Elsie Mackay. Thanks must also go to my friends and family who originally encouraged me to turn my obsessional research into my first book.

Author Biography

Jayne Baldwin divides her time between writing, publishing, running the children's bookshop in Wigtown, Scotland's National Booktown, and teaching yoga. She lives by the sea in Galloway, south west Scotland, and is a director of Curly Tale Books Ltd.